D1743734

FROM BLERIOT TO SPITFIRE

Flying the historic aeroplanes of the Shuttleworth Collection

Compiled and edited by DAVID OGILVY
With specialist contributions from
> *ROLAND BEAMONT*
> *JOHN LEWIS*
> *DICKY MARTIN*
> *DESMOND PENROSE*
> *THOMAS GUTTERY*
> *ALLEN WHEELER*
> *NEIL WILLIAMS*

and a foreword by
MARSHAL OF THE ROYAL AIR FORCE LORD ELWORTHY

Airlife Publications
England

An AIRLIFE publication in the SHUTTLEWORTH series

First Published 1977

©

The Shuttleworth Collection 1977

ISBN 0 9504543 4 6

Airlife Publications

7 St. John's Hill, Shrewsbury, England.

Printed by Livesey Limited, Shrewsbury, England.

Foreword

**Marshal of the Royal Air Force,
the Right Honourable Lord Elworthy,
G.C.B., C.B.E., D.S.O., M.V.O., D.F.C., A.F.C.**

This book analyses the development of the flight and control characteristics of aeroplanes from 1909 to 1939, from the Bleriot to the Spitfire, both single engine, single seat monoplanes. The clear theme emerges that the early pioneers were gravely handicapped by lack of engine power with the result that their aircraft were of light and flimsy structure and capable only of very low speed.

During World War I the pressing demand for higher speed and greater manoeuvrability could only be met by more engine power and its provision enabled heavier and more rigid aircraft to be built and thus capable of being more positively and effectively controlled. The famous Sopwith range of fighters, the Bristol Fighter and the SE5a demonstrated the improvements in control that could be achieved and were major steps towards the more sophisticated systems of the 1930's. With engine power around the 1,000 hp mark and much higher speeds attainable, aircraft structures, then almost exclusively biplanes, had to be made more rigid. Finally, with the Hurricane and the Spitfire, the monoplane came into its own again and it too had to be made rigid.

Bearing this in mind, readers will appreciate the value of the impressions of pilots who not only fly these aeroplanes today but in some cases flew them in their operational days as well. Some of the aeroplanes described, such as the Avro 504K, the Bristol Fighter, the Gloster Gladiator and the Supermarine Spitfire, are among the most famous of all time. Not all the aeroplanes described are military in origin for the de Havilland Moth was probably the best known of all mass produced light sporting civil types, while the Bleriot dates back to the first crossing of the English Channel by a heavier than air flying machine.

Because of the Shuttleworth Collection's unique ability to keep these early aeroplanes in flying condition, we hope this book will be a useful work of reference on some of the most historically significant flying machines produced in the first half-century of aircraft development.

Norman Tower,
Windsor Castle,
Berkshire.

Elworthy

Contents and Authors

The Publishers wish to acknowledge the photographers, to whom all correspondence regarding the photographs should be addressed.

Messrs. Air Portraits of 131 Welwyndale Road, Sutton Coldfield, West Midlands, for the photographs on:-

Pages: 3, 4, 11, 27 Top, 35 Top, 36 Bottom, 43 Top, 61 Top, 69 Top, 77, 83, 89, 97 Top, 103 Bottom, 109, 115, 123, 131, 139 Top, 150 Top, 157, 165.

J. E. Hoad Esq., for the photographs on:-

Pages: 28, 35 Bottom, 36 Top, 43 Bottom, 44, 51, 52, 62, 70, 78, 90, 97 Bottom, 98, 103 Top, 104, 110, 116, 124, 132, 139 Bottom, 140, 149, 150 Bottom, 158, 166.

Ministry of Defence R.A.E. Farnborough, for the photographs on:- Page 84.

The publishers wish to thank the Editor and Authors for their help and would like to point out that all Royalties from sales of the book will go to the Shuttleworth Collection and not to individual authors.

Introduction

The Shuttleworth Collection is the only organisation of its kind in the world. In 1928 Richard Shuttleworth, who was the son of a rich landowning family living at Old Warden Park in Bedfordshire, started his hobby of acquiring early road vehicles. His aim was not to establish a museum, but to assemble a range of historic cars that could be made to work; as proof that they did so, he placed regular entries in the annual London-to-Brighton veteran car run and in other sporting events.

By the early thirties Mr Shuttleworth had learned to fly; in 1932 he acquired one of the original de Havilland Moths, which were by far the most popular and successful light aeroplanes of the time. Although it was only four years old on arrival at Old Warden, with the passing of time this machine became historic. Today it has the claim to have lived on one aerodrome for longer than any other active aeroplane in the history of aviation.

In the period immediately before World War II, Richard Shuttleworth obtained a valuable collection of both cars and aeroplanes, with the 1909 Bleriot, 1910 Deperdussin and 1916 Sopwith Pup among the first of his flying machines. In addition, he carried out many activities in the field of aircraft engineering and, as a Director of the Comper Aircraft Company of Hooton Park, near Liverpool, he flew one of the diminutive single-seat Comper Swifts all the way to India as part of what today would be called a marketing campaign.

In 1940, whilst serving with the Royal Air Force, Richard Shuttleworth was killed in a non-operational flying accident. His historic aircraft and vehicles were in wartime storage and the small aerodrome at Old Warden was used by a civilian contractor repairing some of the lighter types then in service. North American Harvard trainers and Percival Proctor radio trainer/communications machines passed through in substantial numbers. The family house was in use as a military hospital.

After the war the Richard Ormonde Shuttleworth Remembrance Trust was created. The house formed the basis of what is now the Shuttleworth Agricultural College and the aerodrome again became the home of the Shuttleworth Collection. Since then, activities have expanded under a Board of Trustees; today, visitors come from literally all over the world to see the famous aeroplanes that are on display.

A most important aspect of the Collection's activities is that the Trust perpetuates Richard Shuttleworth's original aims. The aeroplanes are not static museum pieces. They fly. But because many of them are the world's sole survivors of their types, they do so under strictly controlled conditions and only when there is good reason. The Trust is an educational charity and hopes to show these valuable veterans in their intended element – the air – for the next and subsequent generations to see. Whilst static study serves a very useful purpose, there can be no substitute for the sight, sound and even the smell of a historic aeroplane in action. Add to this the intentionally timeless atmosphere that has been built-in at Old Warden, with a small all-grass aerodrome in rural surroundings and with an absolute minimum of concrete; then the scene is set for one of the Collection's regular Flying Days on which selected aircraft are publicly demonstrated. Normally these take place on the last Sunday of each summer month, and on some Bank Holidays, often with a specific theme.

Behind the public scene many tasks are carried out. At any time three or four aeroplanes are in the workshops being prepared to take their places on display and bring aviation history to life, while technical and historical research provides answers for enquirers – writers, film makers and others – who have come to regard the Collection as one of the world's main centres for information on early aviation. .

Continuously Old Warden enjoys a controlled expansion. Old aircraft are not obtained *just* because they are old, for each machine selected must have some claim to a place in history. It might not be famous in its own right, but it could mark the beginning or end of a specific era. On the other hand, many of the exhibits are individually world-renowned, such as the Percival Gull in which Jean Batten made her record flights in the mid-thirties, or the de Havilland Comet that won the England-to-Australia air race in 1934. To ensure that the right gaps are filled, the Collection is far from parochial either in outlook or in practice, for a Hawker Hind light bomber was retrieved to its country of origin on a difficult overland journey of 6,000 miles from Afghanistan. The Hind and the Comet are key tasks in the restoration workshops as we put this to press, while a Hawker Hurricane and an Avro Anson are among Shuttleworth machines that are being worked-on by groups in other parts of Britain.

To accommodate the various machines now in the re-storation process, a new exhibition hangar was built during the winter of 1976-77, but to retain the informal spirit of Old Warden, physical development will be strictly contained. The Shuttleworth Collection may be unique, and may have almost limitless scope, but it started as one man's aspiration and the Trustees and staff aim to retain that essential personal element which could be lost through excessive growth. To see what it is like a personal visit is necessary, but if you seek to discover the feeling of flight in the Shuttleworth aeroplanes, hopefully this book provides some of the answers. The wind, the wires and the fresh air in the face may be missing, but personal imagination can go a long way; and, by contrast with the 'real thing', you can go through all this in the warmth of the fireside and the comfort of your favourite armchair.

We have included the majority of the most interesting types. Each author has been chosen because of his specific connection with a particular machine, which in most cases will mean that he has the most experience in flying it and therefore is best suited to give an assessment. Wing Commander Dicky Martin virtually discovered the Gladiator, which originally was built-up from the better parts of two very tired specimens; without his efforts when he was Chief Test Pilot to the Gloster Aircraft Company it is very unlikely that there would be an airworthy Gladiator today. Air Commodore Allen Wheeler learnt to fly in rotary-engined Avro 504Ks in 1925 and still flies the type, so who would be more qualified to write about both the aircraft

Two typical views of a Flying Day.

and its engine? Similar stories apply to other machines and to the pilots who have written about them.

Each author has written in his own style and has been free to express himself as he has wished. An overdose of editing would maim the essential individuality that must go with successful writing, so only a few small changes have been made in attempting to keep a form of free flow through the book.

The book is aimed at all who are interested in historic aeroplanes. Each writer has endeavoured to include sufficient technical material to provide some spice for readers who are pilots and may wish to make comparisons with other types that they know, but at the same time finding a balance that makes sense to someone who is interested without being an active flying person. As most of the machines are sole survivors of their types, many of the chapters that follow may stand in history as the definitive reports on some famous aeroplanes.

Apart from the reports on the individual aircraft, chapters have been included to explain the methods used to manage the early rotary engines and to show the differences between handling machines with fixed tailskids and no brakes and today's designs with tricycle landing gear and steerable nosewheels. One day perhaps a second volume may be justified. At this stage we cannot include articles on the diverse range of types now being restored, such as the Hawker Hind and Hurricane, the Avro Anson, the Parnall Elf and de Havilland Comet, but who knows what may happen in the eighties?

Many may wonder how a pilot becomes privileged to fly the unique aeroplanes of the Shuttleworth Collection. Alas, it is virtually impossible. Regularly, pilots with impressive lists of types flown and with logbooks showing many thousands of hours write to Old Warden begging to be 'allowed in'. Those with worthwhile flying experience, though, will appreciate the need for some form of modest type continuity, so the fewer who fly these machines the better. Some of the aeroplanes in the Collection may fly only three or four times in a year, so clearly these trips should be carried out by one or, at the most, two pilots.

Those who are on the Collection's flying list have been chosen not only for their experience, which in all cases is broad-based, but also for their outlook. All have Service flying backgrounds, and are (or have been) test pilots or flying instructors; some both. The main aim must be to preserve these irreplaceable aeroplanes for as many generations ahead as possible. Taking extreme care in handling both engine and airframe, deciding without argument to cancel a flight if wind and weather are marginal and knowing the significance of placing safety before spectacle are among the qualities required.

Essential though the pilots are, they are as powerless as the aeroplanes would be without the essential skills and efforts of the engineers and craftsmen who make the machines fit to fly. A little about their work appears in the first chapter. However, neither good pilots nor the best engineers can keep these valuable veterans flying without the support of many organisations and individuals in various parts of the world; many airframe components can be made in the workshops, but others, and particularly engine parts, must be found. If you wish to see the historic aeroplanes in the air in future years, please remember this, so if you have an early aero engine in your shed or if you find or hear about any item that may be useful, the staff at Old Warden are always raring to receive the news.

David Ogilvy
Spring 1977

1 *Old aeroplanes do not just happen to fly*   *David Ogilvy*

A visitor to a flying display at Old Warden may well be forgiven for thinking that preparations begin when the hangar doors are opened. The aircraft are pushed outside, then lined-up on the aerodrome to await their turns in the programme. The rather special informal and ageless atmosphere that surrounds these occasions may well add to the flavour of a scene where everything seems so easy; but at the risk of disillusioning those for whom this apparent casualness is a key factor, I will endeavour to put the picture into some balance.

Within recent years, at least, very few 'new' historic aeroplanes have arrived at Old Warden in flying condition. Aircraft selected for addition to the fleet are chosen not because they may be available 'off the shelf', but because they have claims to historical fame or play some significant part in the evolution of the flying machine. For this reason, a representative type may be sought rather than a specific available aeroplane obtained, and if this involves considerable planning, expense and several years' work, the members of the Shuttleworth team are not discouraged.

Let us consider two aircraft of roughly comparable age, each military in origin and each acquired at about the same time – a Hawker Hind and a Miles Magister, both of which reached the peaks of their Service careers in the late thirties. Both types had been on the 'search' list for a few years and everyone seemed to be confident that a Magister could be found. The usual research was set into motion and altogether eight specimens were traced; six were in Britain and two on the Continent. A moderately sound and almost complete example was found in Norfolk, but as it was of wooden construction and had not flown for several years, all the glue joints would be suspect and a fairly extensive stripping and rebuilding sequence would be necessary. Just before it was acquired, though, the world's only flyable Magister became available; within a fortnight, negotiations were completed and its owner flew it into Old Warden.

We hoped for a quick check-over and a repaint in the military markings of the early stages of World War II, but on closer inspection much more work was found to be needed. By Shuttleworth standards, however, the task was a small one and almost exactly a year later it was satisfactorily test-flown. A whole year for an aeroplane that arrived in flying condition? Yes, and when we realise that for the last six months of this time the aeroplane stood in the hangar, complete except for two small rubber seals needed for the undercarriage, the problems and delays associated with even a minor restoration job may begin to break through.

How different has been the story of the Hind. In the late sixties the search that led to this machine's arrival at Old Warden started on a broader base. The Collection sought an operational-type aircraft of the later inter-war era to form a partner to the Gloster Gladiator, which was the only representative on strength. The chosen aeroplane was the biplane Hawker Fury, but none could be found. Imagine the initial disbelief, though, when a story about a hangarful of Hawker Hind light bombers in Afghanistan began to gel. The (then Royal) Afghan Air Force had operated Hinds until 1956, nearly fifteen years after the last specimens had been retired by our own Royal Air Force; instead of scrapping them, the Afghans had put them to bed and left them unscathed except for the deterioration caused by the passage of time.

There *were* Hinds in Afghanistan; detailed investigation soon proved that to be true. But there the problems began. How did one persuade an Air Force 6,000 miles away, operating largely under Russian jurisdiction, to release an aeroplane to what to them must have been a completely unknown collection in England? Correspondence produced no fruit; there was no British Air Attaché in Kabul and the Embassy officials knew nothing about aeroplanes. However, by a very round-about communication process, the Attaché in Teheran agreed to help and in turn he convinced the British

The D.H.88 Comet—Winner 1934 England–Australia Air Race: the biggest restoration task ever undertaken.

The Hawker Hind being restored following its journey of 6,000 miles from Afghanistan.

Secretary in Afghanistan that this was a serious request by a group of people who eventually would restore a Hind to become the world's only surviving flying specimen. Once convinced, the Afghan officials were incredibly co-operative and, subject to certain conditions, agreed to present a complete aircraft to the Shuttleworth Collection. What were those conditions? That it must not be used for commercial gain, or be resold, and that if possible it should fly, at least initially, in the markings of the Royal Afghan Air Force.

Very welcome though the gift would be, how would the Hind be brought home to its country of origin? By this time the aviation grape-vine had been active and surprising numbers of people knew of the problem. Many offers, some fatuous and some realistic, were put to the Old Warden management, but none blossomed into reality. So an offer to provide a suitable covered vehicle, with drivers, plus a coach with medical officer, cook and other support crew was treated as another false start, until I was asked to visit the person making the offer so that he could prove that he meant what he said. When I was ushered to the office of the man in charge of Ford's Dagenham factory, any doubt that may have lingered dispersed almost embarrassingly. Known to us by name, but not by position, he happened to be a member of the Shuttleworth Veteran Aeroplane Society!

The recovery team, with the Collection's then Works Manager as the sole Shuttleworth representative, headed east over a variety of surfaces before reaching Afghanistan, but there the main road to Kabul, which had been laid by the Americans, was found to be in good order. On arrival, the party found that the Afghans had selected the best available parts from the various Hinds and had assembled a complete aeroplane in readiness for a handover ceremony. The Commander-in-Chief of the Air Force, General Gulbahar, confessed to a dose of nostalgia and shed tears as he parted with the aeroplane; he had flown many hours in the Hinds, eighteen of which had been delivered by Britain in two batches: the first new in 1938 and the second, ex-RAF, two years later.

This book is about aeroplanes and the human side of the return overland journey of 12,000 miles cannot justify space here; but one member of the team suffered a heart attack and went to hospital in Turkey, while an outbreak of cholera forced the party to a halt for three weeks on the way home. Three years after the project had been opened, though, the Hind was home in England. Proudly it was assembled and displayed for just one day in the car park of the Headquarters of the Ford Motor Company at Warley, in Essex, and there it became the target for dozens of press cameras. On the next morning the Hind's portrait appeared in no fewer than five national daily papers.

Getting the aeroplane to England had been quite an achievement, but although seemingly complete, it was far from flyable. In later years, no manufacturers' spares had been available and many non-standard components had been incorporated; even sections of Russian packing cases were found in the airframe. Clearly a very major restoration programme was required. Fortunately several firms offered help, and both the radiator and oil cooler were despatched to Serck's for checking and overhaul. The oil cooler returned with a bill of clean health, but the radiator failed a pressure test and was beyond practical redemption. In due course, though, through the joint co-operation of Hawker-Siddeley Aviation and the Royal Air Force Museum, a direct exchange of radiators was made with that in Hendon's Hart. Many mutual-help ventures are carried out between the various aviation collections and museums and the British Aircraft Preservation Council exists largely to encourage such deals.

Meanwhile, in the workshops at Old Warden, the airframe was stripped for inspection. Most of the steel-tube fuselage structure proved to be sound, but various repairs, removal of corrosion, reprotection and repainting were carried out; the wooden formers and stringers, however, could not be salvaged and new sections were made and fitted. Often, in airframe repair tasks, when no drawings are available, a defective component must be built-up to its correct original shape and used as a pattern for making a replacement part. This, of course, is an operation that takes a very considerable amount of time.

Although every practicable effort is made to retain an aeroplane in authentic form, occasionally a small deviation from original may be carried out. A historic aeroplane that is destined to fly must be safe. In the case of the Hind, no parts are available for the early Palmer brakes, so these will be changed for a more modern system, possibly using discs; but despite the amount of work that is put in to restoration and the time needed to complete it, as many original parts as possible are retained. A balance must be struck between authenticity and safety for flight, but so far every historic aeroplane that has emerged from the Old Warden shops has remained largely original. The Hind has a long way to go before it will be ready to fly, but when the great day comes, all concerned in the acquisition and restoration will have cause to be proud of another unique achievement.

Significant though many restoration projects are, none can match that of the de Havilland DH 88 Comet either in technical magnitude or historical importance. Not to be confused with the similarly-named airliner of the early post-war years, the original Comet was a two-seat twin-engined high-performance monoplane designed, built and flown in 1934 to participate in the MacRobertson Air Race from England to Australia. Not only did it start the race little more than nine months after the design first touched the drawing board, but it won against competition from many of the world's other major countries. After its Australia success, the Comet achieved several notable long-distance records and later its unusual wooden construction formed the basis on which the wartime Mosquito was built.

This famous Comet spent nearly all World War II unlovingly parked outside at Gravesend Airport with only a camouflage cover for protection from the enemy and the elements. Many are surprised that it survived at all, but it withstood the time-test sufficiently well to justify being externally refurbished for static display at the Festival of Britain in 1951. After more storage, it was handed over in 1965 by the de Havilland Aircraft Company for custody with the Shuttleworth Collection, and for several years it was on public exhibition. In 1975, however, the Transport Trust (the national body for the preservation and restoration of selected items of historic transport) sought a suitably significant project to adopt. The Comet was put forward and was selected. Since then, apart from the initial funding by the Transport Trust, which set the task in motion, very considerable technical and financial help has been provided by Hawker-Siddeley Aviation as successors to de Havilland.

The Comet story would justify a book of its own. This cannot be written yet, for in addition to the machine's great past, hopefully it has a significant future. Its restoration to flying condition after about forty years on the ground constitutes by far the biggest task of its kind yet tackled by any organisation. The problems are immense, but in addition to Hawker-Siddeley, several other bodies including Hants and Sussex Aviation and British Airways have shown their faith in the project by making practical contributions. Let us leave the Comet for the present in the knowledge that it will be receiving specialist workshop attention for a few more years before it can be ready to fly; but fly it will.

Unfortunately the workshops must remain off stage as far as visitors are concerned. At any time, usually with four or five aeroplanes undergoing restoration or periodic overhaul, the sheer volume of work to be done must call for a minimum of disturbance to the scheduled programme. Because of the nature of the work, with no spares available for drawing from stores, with a need to repair (or make a replacement for) every worn or damaged item and a demand for the accuracy of a craftsman's skill, restoration takes very much longer than the time needed to build a new aeroplane from drawings and new materials. Parts made in the workshops range up to mainspars and even propellers, but such items as tyres, which are impossible to obtain for some wheel sizes, must come from specialist trade sources. Where manufacturers' tyre moulds have been destroyed, the only possible course is to change the wheels to the nearest size for which covers can be made. This in itself may generate other problems.

The team at Old Warden is small. In fact, despite world-wide activities in the field of historical research, liaison, information and so on, the total paid strength numbers only twenty-two. This includes those whose duties cover administration and management, library and research, reception and sales, repairs and maintenance to the buildings and aerodrome as well as the technical requirements. To keep the essential traditional skills alive for generations ahead, a small-scale apprenticeship scheme is in operation, but Wally Berry, the Chief Engineer, heads a force of only six full-time engineers and craftsmen engaged on aircraft work, with two more on vehicle re-storation. A few willing volunteers provide special assistance in their spare time, but clearly these must be very carefully vetted if they are to be entrusted with work on 'living' exhibits.

So remember, please, that when you see a historic aeroplane in the air, it is not there just by chance. It may be flying as a result of several years of search, investigation and restoration by a rather special team attached to an equally special organisation. There is – and can be – only one Shuttleworth Collection.

2 *What is so different about handling an early aeroplane?*
David Ogilvy

The flying qualities of individual aircraft are covered in the reports that follow, so in this chapter we generalise on some of the features that differ between ancient and modern types. Some machines are virtual laws to themselves and in this category must fall the Boxkite, but similar principles apply to them all and it is the way in which such principles affect aeroplanes of differing shapes and sizes that concerns us now.

This is not a lesson on theory of flight. Too many books and articles have been written on this subject to warrant going over the well-worn aerofoils, airflow, lift/drag ratios and so on all over again, but for those who wish to learn – or relearn – these 'basics', some advice appears at the end.

Starting a relatively modern aero engine is almost invariably achieved by the use of an electric starter motor, triggered into action from the cabin by pressing a button on or near the instrument panel. Most light types rely on their internal power supply for this, but the larger engines cause a heavy drain on a small aircraft battery and the usual practice is to plug-in an external trolley-accumulator. The Supermarine Spitfire and Gloster Gladiator are examples of this to be seen at Old Warden. Another method, confined to aircraft with military origins, is to have cartridge starters and these are literally fired into life; for this see the Percival Provost in action.

The engines of earlier aircraft are usually swung by hand. For this the propeller is set to a position just ahead of a compression and on the word 'contact' is swung through that compression as the relevant piston passes through top dead centre. Hopefully it fires. Care is needed to ensure that if the engine kicks back the swinger's fingers are clear of the backward revolving propeller. With larger engines such as the Rolls-Royce Falcon in the Bristol Fighter, two or even three people need to link hands to combine sufficient strength to master the resistance of the compression. In this case the usual verbal instruction is 'one, two, three – go'.

There were a few early aids to success to ease the muscles and to relieve the human hand. The first successful mechanical device was the Hucks starter, on which a long arm projecting from the front of a vehicle connected to a dog on the aircraft propeller, power being provided via the clutch and a chain drive from the vehicle's engine. The world's only known working Hucks exists at Old Warden and occasionally this is used to activate the Bristol Fighter, Avro 504K or Tutor. Another method used extensively in the twenties and early thirties was the starter-mag, which in effect was a third magneto (aero engines are required to have two for normal running as a safety precaution against ignition failure) connected to a hand-crank. An engineer outside and the pilot inside can be seen today practising this rather tiring winding operation on the Avro Tutor and the Hawker Tomtit.

Once an engine is running, different units require different tactics. A rotary objects to prolonged ground running as it tends to suffer quickly from fouled plugs, so in this case a take-off is started as soon as is practicable; but some engines are more sensitive than others to oil temperature and on a cool day Armstrong-Siddeley radials, in particular, may require up to eight minutes at about 1,000 r.p.m. before the minimum figure is reached for a safe run-up and power check. Differing yet again we have the Rolls-Royce Merlin in the Spitfire, the early marks of which have only one radiator, partially blanked by an undercarriage leg, thus causing the coolant to climb to boiling temperature even on a short taxy to the take-off point. To overcome this problem the undercarriage must be retracted as soon as possible after lift-off, but not *too* soon!

Control of an aeroplane when manoeuvring on the ground, or taxying, is very straightforward in a modern aeroplane. The tricycle undercarriage keeps the tail in the air and thus offers a good forward view over the nose; a steerable nosewheel, connected to the rudder pedals, calls for nothing more than application of the left or right foot to control a turn. Closing the throttles and applying the brakes will bring the machine to a stop almost at once – provided, of course, that this ease of operation does not tempt the occupant to move too fast, which unfortunately does happen.

The fin and rudder at the back of an aeroplane act as a weathercock, so the machine always wishes to face into wind. Taxying directly against the wind, therefore, creates no problem, but who wants to do this all the time? The earlier aircraft has no brakes, so its speed cannot be checked quickly. Success in turning depends wholly on the effect of the wind – or more usually the propeller slipstream – on the rudder. So, to turn, we must apply increased power to provide that artificial wind, but by doing so we risk moving more rapidly and we have nothing with which to stop! Therefore, turning in a confined space is impracticable and here a wing man is needed; his task is not just to hold onto the wingtip and act as a standing passenger, but to become a human brake, pulling back on the inside of a turn but releasing the pressure before the pilot achieves his desired heading. Because the tail-down attitude means that the nose must be high, restricting the forward view, the pilot must weave throughout the taxying operation, looking to the right as he turns left and vice versa.

There are several trade-tricks that go with the successful operation of early aircraft, but the associated skills are dying rapidly. When taxying downwind, a turn to a crosswind heading (which, incidentally, is difficult to maintain because of the weathercocking tendency already mentioned) may present problems. The wind from behind and the small amount of slipstream from the propeller of a well-throttled engine may negate each other, with the result that the rudder has no effective airflow round it. Increased power will help, but this will cause an unwanted increase in speed over the ground, so here the ailerons are brought into use. A downgoing aileron will catch a wind from behind and will help to move that side of the aircraft forward, or help on the outside of a turn, so a pilot wishing to turn left applies left rudder, at the same time giving a short burst of engine to generate some slipstream, and using left aileron as an aid. If he is taxying the other way, or into the wind, he uses rudder in the direction of the desired turn, a controlled burst of power and *opposite* aileron, i.e. left rudder and right aileron. Few pilots today know this and the other peculiarities of the vintage art.

Even take-off is different. With a nosewheel aeroplane, a small amount of rudder may be needed in order to help straight against the effect of the slipstream on one side of the aircraft, but otherwise all that is needed is to open the throttle and lift-off at the appropriate speed. With a brakeless tail-wheel type more manoeuvring space will be needed for lining-up accurately, although there should be no problem in facing the correct way for the start of an into-wind take-off. More rudder will be needed, not only to counteract the slipstream, but to fight the gyroscopic effect when the tail lifts and the machine adopts the flying attitude. Cross-wind take-offs are not easy except in very light winds, but then the use of adequate rudder needs to be balanced with use of into-wind aileron in order to keep laterally level during the ground run.

On the climb, at a relatively slow airspeed, when control effectiveness is poor, a fair rudder pressure needs to be maintained to achieve what in today's terms is called balanced flight, which means keeping the top (slip or skid) needle in the middle. Which rudder is needed depends on the direction in which the engine rotates.

Perhaps in turns the greatest difference shows between techniques needed for flying ancient and modern types. Many a machine today will go round a tolerably acceptable turn on aileron alone, although a touch of into-turn rudder is required to achieve flight balance. In an earlier machine, though, an attempt to turn on aileron alone produces quite drastic effects. Bank will come on and an internal gale will hit the pilot on the side of the face, but the aeroplane will show little sign of changing heading. If it does so at all, it may well go the wrong way, for a downgoing aileron creates much more drag than its opposite counterpart and this applies especially to the oldest designs where that down movement is most marked. By the twenties many types had differential ailerons, which means that the upgoing surface moves further than the downgoing control, thus reducing what is known as aileron drag, but with the earlier designs the amounts of up and down travel were identical. So rudder plays a very important part in turning any biplane, on which one of the best ways of testing a pilot's overall co-ordination is to ask him to do a series of turns in opposite directions, rolling straight from one into the other without pausing in the level attitude. If he can keep the slip needle central throughout, he is either good or very lucky!

In the main, biplanes loop happily and with no special problems, but varying amounts of rudder are needed with different types to counteract torque and slipstream effects on the way over. When approaching the top, with full power and a rapidly reducing airspeed, fairly extensive but carefully controlled use of rudder is required. The slow roll, on the other hand, is relatively modern manoeuvre and it was not a practical, popular or fashionable thing to do in the early days. By the very nature of their design *most* biplanes are resistant to roll, while varying amounts of aileron drag at stages on the way round call for equally varied use of the rudder. I cannot imagine anyone successfully slow (as opposed to barrel) rolling the Bristol Fighter and out of respect for its age no pilot today would try; there are exceptions, though, and some of the later and more rounded biplanes, such as the Stampe, are nearer to a monoplane in both feel and control response.

The approach and landing combine to produce an interesting exercise. Effective flaps, a tricycle undercarriage and no wind in the face made one American manufacturer claim that one had just to 'drive up' or 'drive down' in his machine, aiming of course, to compare it with an automobile. Clearly such a claim is dangerous, for any aeroplane, however easy to fly, incorporates built-in hazards for the unwary; but compared with aeroplanes of earlier eras, the modern device *is* driven down. Assuming reasonably calm conditions and plenty of space ahead, it is possible to set-up an approach speed (in itself not very critical) combined with a rough descent rate and then wait until the aircraft touches the ground, finally cutting the throttle and using some brake. This is not the correct way to land a tricycle type, which should be flown to a point near the ground and held-off for a landing on the mainwheels only, but it is possible to arrive on the ground in some safety without excercising many skills.

What do we do with our biplane? At one time there was a fine for any pilot who failed to reach the desired touch-down spot, on three points, after a glide approach all the way in. Apart, perhaps, from the compulsory three-pointer, this applied not just to people in Moths but also to pilots of heavy bombers! This, of course, provided excellent and continuous training for forced landings. Today hardly anyone minds much if a pilot uses a touch of throttle to correct an undershoot on the approach, but judgment still plays a key part. Without flaps, even on a high-drag biplane, the approach angle is fairly flat and the only way to hive-off surplus height is to sideslip; for this almost dead art, one wing is lowered and opposite rudder applied to prevent the nose from falling, thus presenting a 'dirty' aeroplane to the oncoming airflow and steepening the descent angle. It is important to remember to recover to a normal flight condition well before the lowered wing-tip crumples on the ground!

Nearly every early aeroplane should be landed into wind, or with only a minimal cross-wind component. It is important to judge the approach carefully to come in at the correct speed and, where appropriate, to trim-out any fore-or-aft load. Then all is set for the hold-off. If a cross-wind landing is unavoidable, the nose of the aircraft is headed slightly into the wind so that the machine tracks (but does not face) along the desired approach/landing path. At the appropriate stage of the round-out, *just* before touchdown, the drift is kicked off with rudder so that momentarily the machine is both facing and moving in the intended landing direction.

A three-point landing calls for practice. The hold-off needs to be started from the correct final approach speed or, if too fast, 'ballooning' will result. A gradual backward movement of the stick, increasing in rate as the speed decreases and as the elevators lose their effectiveness, should lead to a touch-down on the mainwheels and tail-skid together. If the machine comes off the ground from this attitude, usually it is through no fault of the pilot, for it can be caused only by a sudden gust or rough ground. If a machine lands with its tail off the ground, still with surplus flying speed, and then lifts off in a bounce or balloon, the pilot may well be the culprit.

When landing straight into wind, or in no wind, the early stages of the run call for only minor rudder movements to keep straight, but as the airspeed decreases and rudder effectiveness diminishes, very rapid and energetic footwork may be needed. The final stages of a run made into a wind of, say, ten knots, are much easier than into a dead calm, for in the first case there is some airflow over the rudder even when the machine is stationary.

Without brakes, the last part of a cross-wind (or dead calm) landing may become unmanageable. The rudder, which provides the only directional control available, has no effect, so even a most experienced and competent pilot may finish the run with a swing or, if this cannot be checked, even a ground loop. This occurs because on a tail-down type the centre of gravity must be behind the mainwheels and when the swing starts the momentum is such that the bulk of the weight tends to push ahead, thus aggravating the swing. Apart from imposing an excessive sideload on the undercarriage, this can lead to the outside wing digging-in and, of course, considerable embarrassment for the unfortunate pilot. Most swings are readily correctable by prompt action, but occasionally one may be totally unavoidable.

Apart from the handling aspects, flying in vintage style has many attractions, some of which cannot be easily pinpointed or defined. A slow, open biplane may not be the best mount for trying to go from one place to another into a strong wind on a very cold day, but what can be more pleasant than the DH 60 Moth at eight o'clock on a warm, calm, clear June evening? The aim need not be to go somewhere, but just to enjoy the pure pleasures of flying for flying's sake, which reveal themselves in retrospect even more than at the time. Ten minutes in one's chosen aeroplane in the right conditions are worth more than ten hours in a device that may be an efficient travel tool but nothing more.

In the period leading to World War II, the greater power available from developed and supercharged engines obviously led to higher speeds. This in turn removed any 'slop' that might have existed in the earlier, slower aircraft types and made controls stiffer, but more responsive. Clearly with a wider diversity of airspeeds between the top of the scale and, say the landing approach or when near the stall, problems arose with maintaining good qualities of 'feel' throughout the range; however, various forms of control balancing, leading later still on some types to such devices as spring tabs, helped to reduce the difference. Perhaps the Percival (piston) Provost of the early fifties, a specimen of which exists in the Shuttleworth Collection, is one of the best examples of an aeroplane with nicely harmonised controls that feel right at all speeds.

To those readers who have pilots' licences, let me save you the time and postage by adding that there is no hope of flying the aeroplanes of the Shuttleworth Collection, but the chance to fly something different from your usual mount might well arise. Fortunately several Tiger Moths have survived and these are housed at various aerodromes all over Britain and, indeed, abroad. If you know someone who owns one you may be fortunate enough to glean a trip. You will not regret it; but please remember that it is not a toy to be treated with contempt. It calls for airmanship and handling skills a bit beyond those needed for most modern light aeroplanes, so be prepared to take guidance – and enjoy it!

Any reader wishing to learn more about the theory of flight is advised to study the standard book of reference: 'Flight without Formulae', by A. C. Kermode. Anyone wishing to delve more deeply should see 'Mechanics of Flight' by the same author.

To find a little more about the basic principles of handling an aeroplane, 'Flying Light Aircraft' (A. & C. Black) or 'Flying Facts' (Lernhurst) both by David Ogilvy, may be useful. To learn about a specialist art in the air, 'Aerobatics' (Airlife) by Neil Williams will provide the answers. Also of interest are: 'Flying Between the Wars' and 'Building Aeroplanes for Those Magnificent Men' (Foulis) both by Air Commodore A. H. Wheeler.

More detailed technical and historical descriptions of the aeroplanes in this book are contained in the Shuttleworth Collection official guide, compiled by Wing Commande T. E. Guttery, the Collection's Honorary Archivist.

3 *Operating a rotary engine*
Air Commodore A. H. Wheeler

A rotary engine as referred to in relation to aeroplanes is one in which the whole engine crank-case, cylinders, valves, pistons and connecting rods all rotate round the stationary crank shaft which itself is firmly fixed to the engine bearer plate on the fuselage. The propeller is bolted to the crank case of the engine. This brief description of the rotary engine is given because an entirely new type of engine has now been developed for cars which is often called a rotary but works on a very different principle.

The original reason for the development of the rotary engine for aeroplanes, in about 1909 in its earliest form, was to get over two fundamental problems in using the existing car engines: they were very heavy mainly because they needed a flywheel and they tended to overheat because they had to be run continuously at almost full power with a minimum of cooling, to save both weight and drag. By making the engine itself rotate one had a magnificently heavy fly-wheel and the cooling of the cylinders was assured even when the aeroplane was stationary. Problems were involved with this arrangement but they were not insuperable.

Firstly the air and fuel had to be got into the engine and this could only be done through the hollow crankshaft with a somewhat primitive carburettor. There was, however, one range of engines which supplemented the air supply by allowing the exhaust valve to remain open during the induction stroke and the pure air thus sucked in mixed in the cylinder with a very rich mixture which got in through holes in the cylinder skirt which were uncovered when the piston reached the inward end of its stroke. The best known of this range of engines was the Monosoupape (Mono for short) which became the standard engine in the Avro 504Ks used in the Royal Air Force.

Oil was also fed in through the hollow crankshaft to the bearings. To prevent the oil being washed off the moving surfaces by the fuel it was normal to use a pure vegetable oil (castor) which is not diluted by petrol. There is a 'pulsator' glass dome on the dash-board which indicates when the oil is flowing correctly: the oil should be about half-way up the glass.

Although fairly high centrifugal stresses were imposed by the engine rotation, reciprocating stresses on the connecting rods were eliminated completely. The major stress involved was due to gyroscopic 'kicks' due to any rapid manoeuvres in the air: these had to be contained by the hollow crankshaft and main bearings and thus passed on to the airframe.

Although the 50 hp Gnome engine installed in the 1912 Blackburn Monoplane has three levers controlling the carburation many of the early rotaries had only one. However, the later rotaries dating from the mid-war years (1916) had more sophisticated forms of carburettor which provided some control over the power at both ends of the range. This was a help towards achieving low idling power but became almost essential at high power for flying in formation. These carburettors had two control levers: one controlled the air supply by a single large shutter and the other was virtually a fuel tap but designed to give a very fine adjustment to the fuel supply – it was called the 'fine adjustment'. With this arrangement the pilot had a certain amount of control over the engine speed and power but at best only about 25% with smooth running, and perhaps another 20% by weakening the mixture to get the intermittent 'brrpp-brrpp' running associated with all rotary engines on very low power. Basically, and for all normal flights, not in formation, pilots used full power. Advantages of this system of carburation were that there was a 'built-in' mixture control for high altitudes or for variations in the pressure in the fuel tank, and slight variation due to static (ground) running as opposed to running in the air when the pressure at the air inlet varied slightly – hence the reason for keeping the mixture on the weak side on take-off. It was also unlikely to get icing in the carburettor because nearly all the carburation took place inside the crankcase. This also helped to cool the engine.

Disadvantages were that the pilot himself had to find the right fuel/air mixture for the engine by manipulating the two levers – or the one lever in the case of the Mono. Just pushing the levers further forward does not necessarily give more power, indeed it is more likely to make the engine cut out due to over-richness of the mixture. One sure sign of over-richness is black smoke pouring out behind but the pilot doesn't see that. Another sign is falling off of engine power: this could be due to an oiled-up plug which is usually noticed due to rough running, or a weak mixture which is usually very noticeable because of the 'brrpp-brrpp' which results from a very weak mixture. It is for this reason that a pilot who suspects loss of power should first assume over-richness and close the fine adjustment: the engine may then take a little time to recover since the crankcase may have got a lot of surplus fuel sloshing about inside it. In bad cases of over-richness the engine can take up to about seven seconds to recover. This emphasises the importance of a pilot NOT getting the engine too rich on take-off. Experienced pilots normally 'feel' back the fuel lever at frequent intervals to make sure the mixture has not got too rich. If the mixture is too weak recovery is immediate when the fuel lever is pushed forward.

There are two different methods of starting a rotary engine, but in either case the pilot must first of all see that the fuel tank is pressurised to approx. $2\frac{1}{2}$ lbs. pressure – with the fuel and fine adjustment shut off: he must also check that the switch (or switches) are off. The early rotaries had only one magneto but later ones mostly had dual ignition.

One method of starting up is to turn the engine forwards and squirt a little fuel into each cylinder when the exhaust valve opens: that means two complete turns of the engine. The engine is then given one or two turns till the propeller is in a convenient position for swinging and one cylinder is beginning the compression stroke. All this time both the fuel and air lever are closed but the main petrol tap can be turned on during the priming operation. The ground crew then call out 'switches on'; the pilot replies 'contact'. The ground crew then swing the prop. If the engine fires on swinging the pilot pushes both levers forward for about $\frac{2}{3}$ of the quadrant and then adjusts the engine running to the dot-and-go-one 'brrpp-brrpp' indicating a weak

mixture at the nearest one can get to an idling speed. It is important that the pilot takes care in pushing the levers forward so that he 'catches' the engine before it uses up the fuel it had in the cylinders and crankcase but does not choke it with too much fuel. The engine can also be controlled by the ignition ('blip') switch but control by the fuel lever is better since it gives the pilot the feel of that control and is a rather lesser strain on the engine: it is also much more 'professional'!

If the engine does not start on the swing the pilot switches off, calls out 'off' and keeps the two levers closed. The ground crew then turn the engine to the next suitable position, on compression, and ready for swinging. A good swinger is an essential member of the ground crew, i.e. one who can achieve at least 180° follow through which turns the engine over two compressions. Swingers have been known who threw the prop round 360°!

The other method of starting up differs from the previous method only in the priming stages. In this method, which was used in the Royal Air Force with the Mono engine, the pilot saw that the switch was off, the fuel tank was pressurised to $2\frac{1}{2}$ lbs. and the main fuel tap was on and then, on request from the ground crew, pushed the (single) fuel lever forward till the fuel ran out of the open valve of the bottom cylinder: then the ground crew called out 'petrol off' and the pilot shut the 'fine adjustment'. The ground crew then called out 'sucking in' and turned the engine over (forwards) for about three turns: procedure then followed the same sequence as described before – propeller at convenient position for swinging with one cylinder coming on to compression .... 'contact'.

After the pilot has got the engine running at minimum idling speed with the two levers (fuel and air) adjusted as far back as possible the engine can be allowed to warm up: this takes less than half a minute. The pilot then makes certain that one of the ground crew is leaning over the fuselage near the tailplane to prevent the aeroplane being pulled over on to its nose at full power: then he advances the two levers till he gets full power taking care to keep the air lever well ahead of the fuel lever to prevent over-richness. It is at this stage that the beginner should take the opportunity to familiarise himself completely with the handling of the engine by trying the setting of the levers on full power and making minor adjustments to ensure he has got full power. When he is certain of this setting he should note the positions of the two levers on the numbered quadrant so that he can get it immediately on take-off. A rotary engine is not prone to overheating when run up on the chocks but excessive running under this condition should be avoided.

When this has been done the pilot pulls back the air and fuel levers to a low power setting (idling) and waves away the chocks indicating to the ground crew that he is ready to taxi out. The ground crew then pull the chocks away from the wheels but still remain at the wing tips. The man at the tail stands clear. In conditions of light wind no assistance will be needed from the ground crew in taxying so they may also be waved away and the pilot proceeds to taxy as indicated in chapter 7.

It should be mentioned here that the rotary engine in the Shuttleworth Trust's Avro 504K is a 110 hp le Rhone which is one of the later types of rotaries with a two lever mixture control but with single ignition. The Clerget rotary was one of the most highly developed rotaries with two lever mixture control and dual ignition. A Clerget will be fitted to the Sopwith Triplane now under construction for the Collection by Northern Aeroplane Workshops.

4 The Bleriot XI

John Lewis

The collection owns a genuine Bleriot Type XI, built in 1909 by Louis Bleriot himself. The aircraft is in wholly original condition, aside from having been recovered, and having a small main undercarriage modification; and has its original Anzani 3 cylinder motor. The aircraft has been in Shuttleworth hands since 1935 and has been maintained in flying condition since 1936, when it was flown by Richard Shuttleworth himself at the Royal Air Force Display. Since then it has appeared at many air displays both before and after the Second World War.

Because of the lower power and the uncertainty that the motor will continue to run for more than a couple of minutes at full power, the flying of the aircraft is limited to hops lasting the length of the airfield only. Let us now look at this fascinating machine in detail, and see what a typical flight consisting of three of these hops is like.

The aircraft is a wire-braced monoplane, with single tail and rudder surfaces. The wings are heavily cambered and are supported by king posts above and below the centre section. Through this structure also go the wires which are used to warp the wings for lateral control. The fuselage is an open lattice construction of wood, wire braced; and the pilot sits in a splendidly uncomfortable wickerwork seat just abeam the wing trailing edge. As a concesssion to decency, the sides and bottom of the fuselage are covered with a loose canvas snap-on cover as far back as the seat, but aft of this, where side covers would help to supplement directional stability, they are absent. There is no fin, and the rudder is extremely small. The tailplane is unusual in that it also has heavy positive camber and that the inboard portion is fixed. The elevators are mounted outboard of this fixed portion and comprise the whole tip each side. They are hinged roughly at mid-chord and have a very large range of movement. The undercarriage is a tailwheel design, with bungee springing, and has the unusual feature that all three wheels castor freely, against a light spring force.

The pilot's controls are a little peculiar to the modern eye, but they work in a conventional fashion. The control column is pivoted at its base, and moves in the normal sense for lateral and longitudinal control, but to confuse the issue it has a large fat-rimmed wheel mounted flat on top, which has no function other than to act as a handgrip, and does not turn or do anything else interesting. The rudder bar is smooth wood with no foot restraint, and operates over an uncomfortably large range, so that in use the pilot risks sprained ankles, or worse still a loss of control when one foot slips completely off. What passes for the throttle is mounted on the right hand side of the control column, beneath the wheel, and is, in fact, the ignition advance and retard. This works in the reverse sense from normal in that pulling it aft towards the pilot increases power, and vice versa. To complicate the issue it has a ratchet which locks it on and which has to be released before power can be reduced. This successfully governs the motor from a slow tickover at about 300 rpm to its maximum of about 1,000 rpm; at which in its present condition it yields just about enough of its nominal 25 bhp to lift the aircraft off the ground and to fly at about 10 feet in ground effect.

The motor is a three cylinder fan formation, with the included angle of the outside pair roughly 120°. Construction is approximate, to say the least, and the angle between each barrel and its neighbour is different, which makes timing something of a problem. Lubrication is by a total loss castor oil system, fed through an adjustable feed cock and sight glass, from a pressurised tank. The tank pressure is pilot-generated by a hand pump, and of course, feed rate tends to vary with pressure; although the aim, if a hand can be spared, is to maintain 2 psi. Each cylinder barrel has a ring of ventilation holes cut about half way down the stroke, so that the exhaust gases can be vented direct to the air, in addition to a normal exhaust pipe from the head. This feature, intended to supplement the inadequate exhaust valves, is useful in that combustion can be seen, and mixture strength thereby checked, and very nearly lethal in that it guarantees that the pilot operates throughout in a haze of castor oil mist and exhaust fumes. Having extremely uneven firing intervals, the motor has to have an enormously heavy crankshaft cum flywheel, in addition to the propeller, and even with this the vibration level is high. However, the airframe is so flexible that this scarcely matters in the structural sense, but the pilot is aware of it from time to time as his vision blurs perceptibly. An exhaust valve lifter, necessary to stop the motor, an ignition switch and a fuel cock quite out of the pilot's reach complete the cockpit picture. Note, if you will, that no instruments at all are fitted aside from the tank pressure gauge.

The first problem that faces the Bleriot pilot is how to get in. The one footstep provided is way out of reach, and every time he leans on the aircraft or catches hold of it to try to climb in, it is apt to sidle away on its castoring undercarriage. Getting in is one of the most difficult parts of the flight, and one sometimes wonders if it ought not to be made impossible. A ladder and a helpful engineer are the solution, however, and once in only the discomfort, exposure and the fact that most things are out of reach are disconcerting. The next stage, the ritual of starting, can now begin.

Since the carburettor is always full open, liberal flooding is necessary together with priming into the inlet ports, before a start can be considered likely. The trembler coil ignition is then connected to its batteries, and the prop turned over a few blades to suck the mixture in. Meantime, to take his mind off the fuel pouring out of the carb, the pilot pressurises the oil tank, checks that oil begins to flow into the sight glass, and sets the advance and retard about $\frac{1}{3}$ from the most retarded position. The prop is now set carefully on compression, and, on a call of 'contact' from the engineer doing the start, the pilot switches on the single ignition switch. The prop is swung and, if everything has been done correctly, and the old girl feels like it, the motor fires and we are in business. A blast of cold air comes back from the propeller and at once the pilot has to lower his goggles. Shortly after, the first of the second-hand castor oil begins to arrive in the cockpit area, and the feed is adjusted so as not to oil up the plugs. At this stage the ignition is advanced so as to increase power and make sure that all the cylinders fire

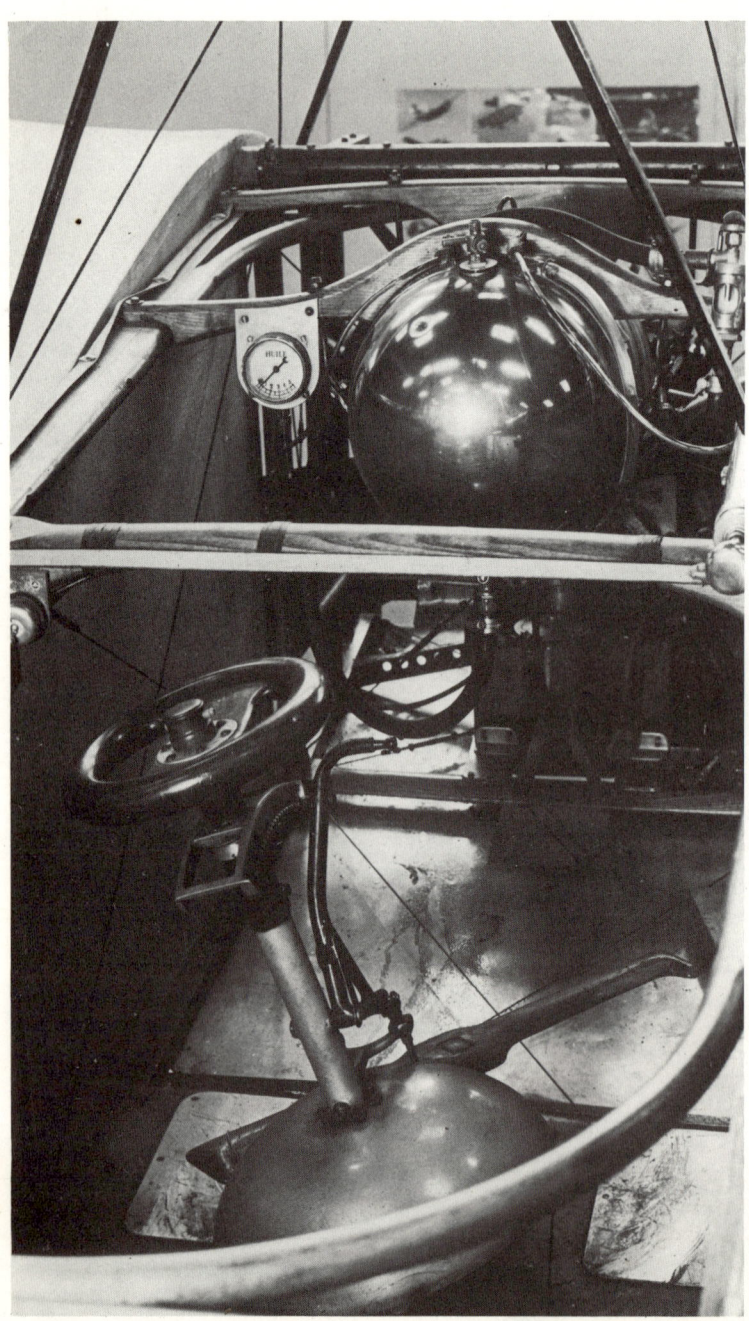

and get warm. For some reason, there is a lazy pot on this Anzani – the starboard one – and if it is run for any length of time from cold on two, the third will never cut in. We then have to stop the motor and change the plug for a hot one and try again. It is better to avoid this rigmarole if possible as there is no guarantee it will fire at all the second time, and the engineers do not like it. Once satisfactorily warmed, however, a brief run-up is done to check by ear that all is well, and again to adjust the oil feed; then power is reduced, the chocks waved away, and we are ready to taxy.

The Bleriot is never flown in winds in excess of 5 knots for reasons of low control power, and for the same reasons we also only taxy in light winds or flat calm. Even so, directional control is so poor that wing handlers are required to do more than taxy in a straight line, or to negotiate any sloping ground. The sloping ground problem arises from the fact that all wheels castor freely, against the weak spring centring system, and so the system generates virtually no side force. Put the aircraft sideways on a slope and it will set off sideways downward at once, unless the pilot can turn it to head up the gradient, and with poor directional control this is often not possible. With understanding handling, the main taxying problem becomes keeping the motor running hard enough to prevent plug-oiling without achieving too high a speed, and not prolonging the process so much that the motor overheats.

Because of the poor directional control, no attempt is made to take off crosswind, irrespective of runway direction. With the aircraft lined up exactly into wind, therefore, one of the handlers holds onto the tail, and the motor is run-up to full power, and the oil pressure and feed-rate checked. When all is to his satisfaction, the pilot raises one arm, holds it out parallel with the ground, then drops it smartly to his side. Upon this signal the handler releases the tail, the aircraft rolls gently forward, and the flight is about to begin.

In the few seconds before the aircraft reaches flying speed, the pilot has an opportunity to check the oil feed and by the clouds of oil rushing past him decide perhaps to vary the rate or not. The decision is a hard one, because time is short and the oil cock very nearly out of reach. Assuming all is well, however, and the pilot can still see through his goggles, the tail is raised as a fast walking pace is achieved, and at a slightly nose up flying attitude the gentle acceleration continues until the aircraft lifts itself off the ground. No airspeed indicator is fitted, but 25 mph is probably a fair estimate of flying speed for this aircraft. Even at this modest pace the airfield looks extremely small, and once a wheel height of 10 feet or more is achieved, smaller still. The first priority is therefore when and how one is going to get it down again, and unless the pilot is careful the first flight is apt to be over before he has had time even to consider the question of how the aircraft handles. The most striking impression of the aircraft is the large elevator hinge moment, in the nose up sense, which requires a constant 10 lb push force on the stick to hold level flight. A moment's inattention and the aircraft will abruptly pitch up, and be a great deal higher and be flying a great deal more slowly than the pilot would wish. Luckily, the elevator control is relatively powerful and precise. This high and slow situation cannot be maintained, however, as the motor gives insufficient power to fly out of ground effect and provided prompt action is taken to prevent a possible stall, no harm is done and the aircraft sinks sedately back down to a wheel height of about 20 feet. By this time most of the airfield will undoubtedly have been used up, and it will be time to land, and to begin the long taxy back to the start point for the next hop. As we have never stalled the aircraft, either deliberately, because we cannot achieve a safe height to do so and because the aircraft is virtually priceless, nor accidentally, nothing is known about its behaviour in this regime.

During the next take-off the pilot notices that the elevator push force develops very early in the roll and that once the tail is lifted, a slight relaxing of this forward pressure will allow the wheels to leave the ground a little earlier than if the aircraft is left to itself, and so save precious distance for the flight. There is a limit to the gain to be had from this technique, however, and should the incidence increase too much, acceleration is slowed and the distance once again increases. The best conditions seem to occur at a point just about when the tailwheel would begin to touch. Once airborne again the heavy vibration is noticed, and a glance at the blurred structure shows just how out of balance the motor is. It is time now, however, to explore the control power, before we run out of airfield, and to see where the limits of controllability might be expected to lie. A small lateral input each way shows that roll power is low, and one rapidly progresses to full deflection, and this yields a delayed and very low roll rate which is also very difficult to stop. At this stage it is apparent that any gust-induced roll disturbance is going to be very difficult to handle, and that some help will clearly be necessary. Therefore rudder inputs are tried, so as to generate sideslip, and to see if this induces a roll rate. The rudder itself is also found to be weak, even with full slipstream over it, and although sideslip does eventually result, the secondary roll rate developed by it is also very low. It is now clear that the major problem axis of the aircraft is the roll, with directional following it a close second, and we redouble our determination not to fly other than in calm conditions. Once again, however, the end of the airfield approaches and it is time to land.

During the taxy back to the other end of the airfield it is apparent that a slight wind has got up, and directional control of the aircraft becomes awkward, giving the handler a hard time keeping the direction constant. Also, the motor is showing signs of overheating, so the oil rate is increased slightly and the tank pressure restored to 2 psi. Fuel is still not a problem, as we started out with 5 gallons, which should last for a couple of hours or more, and the sight glass in the tank confirms this. Now also the continuous exhaust fumes are starting to have an effect, and the pilot is covered with a thin film of castor oil. Before the next hop, the goggles must definitely be cleaned, and it is also decided that this will be the last hop in this series, and that on this mainly the landing will be explored.

In the air again, it is soon obvious that the power from the motor is decreasing and that the first landing is coming up fairly soon, like it or not; and that there may not be power available for a second. Nevertheless, rather than let the aircraft sink on itself, power is reduced, and it is surprising how quickly one has got used to the reversed sense of the power lever. At once the nose pitches up again as the slipstream reduces, and with a smart forward stick input the descent is started. The touch-down follows seconds later, and it is a relief to be able to release the forward pressure on the control column for a second. The geometry of the machine is such that without even trying, a three-point landing results, and there is therefore no need to lower the tail. The disadvantage is that as soon as power is reduced in these circumstances, directional stability also is reduced sharply and controlling the roll-out becomes a full time task. The castoring undercarriage, so soft and gentle in touch-down, now becomes an additional hindrance because even if the aircraft heading can be changed, the lack of sideforce on the mainwheels means that probably the machine will simply crab and maintain its original direction. Opposite wing warp sometimes helps, but in the extreme the pilot has to take refuge in the low speed and just to hope that the thing will stop before he hits anything. In the interests of flight safety we have limited the castoring ability to a fraction of its original value by a wire tie, but the problem still exists.

Power is at once applied again, however, to attempt another hop and landing, and proves to be still sufficient to lift the aircraft a foot or two off the ground. Since distance is very limited, an immediate and final landing is called for, and so for an experiment this time power is abruptly reduced to the idle setting of about $\frac{1}{3}$ advance. The result is an instantaneous speed loss and a much more crisp pitch-up than before. Before there is time fully to counteract this the aircraft has landed again, untidily, a little tail wheel first. Also, a fairly abrupt swing has developed which needs full rudder and a little burst of power to correct, but all is well, and the gentle roll-out is completed some 100 yards short of the boundary, where the handlers turn the aircraft round for the journey back to the flight line. Plainly, the gentle reduction technique is, as expected, the best, and this is obviously the one to be used in the future.

The feeling of well-being and worthwhileness which is always present after a successful flight is never more obvious than now. Not only have we flown, but we have had the unique privilege of flying a genuine Bleriot monoplane, in very nearly the exact configuration and circumstances that Louis Bleriot himself might have done. With all its peculiarities and shortcomings, this has been as it always is, a wonderful experience. It is true that wing warping will never replace the aileron, and that one has been smothered in oil, and breathed exhaust fumes for half the time, but this has not detracted one bit from the delight. One can only be grateful for the experience, and wonder at the courage and resource of a man who could design and build such a machine, and eventually attempt and conquer the Channel in it.

5 The Bristol Boxkite
Neil Williams

One of the only two aircraft in the Shuttleworth Collection that cannot claim to be an original, but one of several machines built for the film 'Those Magnificent Men in their Flying Machines', the Bristol Boxkite reproduction never fails to enthral spectators at a flying display as it sails through the air with the dignity of an old-time sailing ship. What a splendid view the pilot must have, with no cockpit around him, and practically nothing to obstruct downward vision. Yet, because of the seeming fragility of the aeroplane when seen at close quarters on the ground, few spectators would care to become a passenger, although the aeroplane is actually a two seater.

One expects to suffer from vertigo, or agoraphobia; indeed, on first acquaintance, one is reluctant to believe that the contraption can actually fly. It doesn't look like an aeroplane, with its forward booms and foreplane, balanced by the triple rudder and double tailplane, surrounding the pusher propeller. It is a tangled forest of struts, spars, wires, and turn-buckles; commonsense says it cannot fly. But let us suppose that it is a quiet summer's evening, calm, cloudless, with no other flying. The air is warm, but most important, there is no turbulence; as the old pioneers would say, 'There is plenty of lift in the air.' Were there any marked turbulence we would not venture into the air, as the Boxkite might not be able to climb: the early aviators' tales of being 'forced down' were not entirely groundless. We have decided to make a short flight in the vicinity of the airfield, and with no wind we have planned to take off down hill on the longest run available.

Having actually located the pilot's seat, the first obstacle presents itself; how does one board the craft? Help is soon forthcoming, and a ladder is obtained and placed against the leading edge of the bottom right wing. Some care is necessary to negotiate the wires, and it is a good idea to push the control column forward before attempting to sit down. A full safety harness is provided, but the geometry of the shoulder straps makes them very uncomfortable, and one has a better feel for the balance of the machine when they are dispensed with.

On taking hold of the stick, the aviator is disturbed to find that with controls held neutral, the top of the stick is directly in front of his eyes! Since the aileron wires are connected to the stick immediately below the handgrip, it follows that the handgrip must be used in order to exert the necessary leverage. This in turn means that the would-be aviator is committed to peering over or under his arm in order to see where the machine is taking him. At this stage it is a good idea to tuck one's trouser legs into one's socks; even in summertime the draught can be disconcerting!

The instruments are minimal; there is an oil pressure gauge and an airspeed indicator. The most important indicator on the aeroplane is a piece of waxed string tied to a cross-wire beneath the foreplane. The aviator should see that it is securely attached, and that it hangs freely, as this indicates sideslip. In a craft of marginal performance, any sideslip can prevent the machine from climbing, and keeping this string streaming straight back is the key to successful flight.

Pre-starting drill is simple; the petrol tap at the left of the pilot's chair is turned on and the throttle is pumped several times. A voice from somewhere astern cries 'Contact', and the ignition switches are selected on. A loud clatter from the rear of the device announces the fact that the engine has started, and this is confirmed by the rise in oil pressure. While the engine is warming up the flying controls may be tested. At this point one may be excused for having second thoughts as lateral movement of the stick produces no reaction from the control surfaces which hang limply from all four wings. However, by gathering in the slack in the cables festooning the lower wings, one experiences a slight feeling of relief to see that the ailerons can actually be operated when the airflow raises them to the flying position. If doubt still exists, helpers will place the ailerons in the horizontal position, which will allow a practical demonstration.

Next the elevator is tested, and the rear elevator can be seen to operate conventionally, in conjunction with the foreplane. At first, there is a strong tendency to move the stick back and fore whilst looking at elevator and foreplane in turn, as though expecting to catch one of them moving the wrong way. Having experimented with the rudder bar, and found that it is normal in operation, the engine is now sufficiently warm to be run up. There is no tachometer and magnetos are checked by ear. The noise is excruciating at full power; with a pusher propeller the sound is particularly loud and harsh. At idle the engine burbles away happily and one finds it strange to have no slipstream at all to contend with.

The chocks are pulled away and we are ready to taxy. Stick back, and a little power – at this point another snag has arisen; with the stick fully back, the foreplane has rotated until it blots out all forward view from the pilot's chair. A compromise is reached with the stick only slightly back, and as the aeroplane starts to move one is surprised at the smooth ride over rough grass. No modern aeroplane ever had an undercarriage like this. Slowly, and with the dignity of its years, the Boxkite approaches the runway. From the pilot's seat, the sensation is very much like looking down over the bows of a small boat and watching the water flowing past. The aeroplane responds slowly to rudder on the ground, and turns are best made by applying full rudder and using short bursts of engine to swing the machine around.

At last we are ready. The throttle is opened quickly to full power, the engine blaring in a crescendo of sound as the machine lumbers ponderously forward. One is fleetingly conscious of the similarity to boating again as the grass glides past underneath, and out of the corners of one's eyes one becomes aware of wires straightening and tightening as the ailerons begin to trail upwards. The whole machine is vibrating slightly in tune with the engine, but the ride is surprisingly smooth over the rough grass; and we must be doing all of 20 mph by now. Slowly the controls are coming to life, and the aviator can begin to feel the forces of the airflow against the control surfaces. The controls become tighter and stiffer but we are holding them neutral until we have reached a comfortable speed. With a sudden shock, and before we are prepared, the machine is flying! The transition from ground to air was so subtle that it could not be felt. But wait, this is no time for reverie; the foreplane is rising above the horizon and the control column is moving backwards of its own accord. The airspeed, still ridiculously low, is falling further. We ease forward on the stick, and the aircraft dives sharply as the stick snatches forward. Instinctively we pull back and the machine rears up. Now the problem is clear; the aircraft is completely unstable longitudinally, mainly due to the centre of pressure movement on the foreplane. We release the throttle and use two hands on the stick in an attempt to steady it, and this is successful. But now we are approaching the end of the airfield, and we are still only about 10 feet above the ground. The machine is not climbing, and it is too late to stop. We concentrate on keeping the foreplane just above the horizon and snatch a glance at the airspeed indicator – 30 mph. We also observe fleetingly that the throttle is still wide open, and remember gratefully that the throttle nut was tightened before take-off. The machine is difficult to fly – how could the old pioneers possibly have learned to fly in a device like this? We concentrate on holding the correct attitude, and suddenly realise why the machine will not climb. The string attached to the crosswire is blowing sideways, perhaps 20° off line. We are sideslipping, but the slipstream is so low without the propeller blast that its direction cannot be assessed by the pilot. A moment's thought is necessary before deciding which rudder bar to press, and then the string swings across slowly until it points straight back. And slowly, very slowly, we begin to climb. By now we have discovered that by making only very small movements of the elevators it is possible to fly one handed again.

For the first time the aviator is able to look around and survey the countryside. He is amazed and delighted at the view; no other aeroplane can offer a sight like this! We are so slow, and so low, that every minute detail on the ground can be seen; and there is time to study it. We watch someone appear at a farmhouse door, stare unbelievingly, and disappear indoors, only to reappear moments later with the entire family. We risk a wave of the arm which nearly upsets the craft, and with delight and amusement the entire group waves back! Motorists stop and stare and we are fascinated to see a cyclist nearly fall off his bicycle as he gazes upwards. It becomes a game, to wave, and to see how many people one can count waving back. A seagull appears, and with easy grace wheels in a wide arc, and drops into neat formation just off the wingtips, his undercarriage partly extended, acting as airbrakes. After a moment, with an air of disdain and disbelief, his feet disappear neatly and he curves away into the distance while we watch with envy such a perfect demonstration of flight.

Cautiously we start a slow turn to the left, and immediately our precious altitude begins to disappear. The elusive string will not stay in the correct position and the angle of bank is increasing. We attempt to level the wings, but the stick will barely move and the treetops are getting very close. The use of two hands and some considerable force restores level flight again at the expense of some rather unsteady pitching oscillations, but the aeroplane does not begin climbing until that infernal piece of string is back in the centre. A turn to the right is more satisfactory and we remember that the original aeroplane with its rotary engine would barely turn left at all, according to reports.

The aileron control is very heavy, and after ten minutes, piloting the machine has become very tiring. Again, we try a turn, and this time the string remains central. Looking very much like its namesake, the Boxkite curves majestically through the quiet air towards the aerodrome.

We decide to try a glide approach, and pull the throttle right back. The airspeed drops alarmingly, and automatically we push the nose down. But the speed is still falling – we dare not stall this machine; anything might happen. Eventually the speed stabilises at 24 mph, but the angle of dive is very steep indeed. We realise now why the aviators in those early days placed so much emphasis on pushing the nose down in the event of an engine failure. The density of the Boxkite is so low and the drag so high that if the throttle is closed the machine practically stops in its tracks!

We abandon the idea of doing a glide landing and restore half power, a procedure which causes one or two disturbing oscillations in pitch as we once again overcontrol on the elevators.

The approach is surprisingly relaxing, and at 30 mph the machine is flying well. Now that the approach is shallower, we can see the airfield beneath the foreplane again, and as we cross the hedge we have to increase power to maintain the airspeed.

With about $\frac{2}{3}$ power set, and the stick gripped firmly with both hands we are ready for any tricks the landing may spring upon us.

Gently we ease the craft into level flight just above the ground, and slowly it loses speed and begins to settle. While we are still trying to estimate the height of the wheels above the ground, the machine alights, gracefully and softly, all by itself! It is as though, having shown its mettle, it wishes to make amends. It slows to walking speed, as a good aeroplane should, and still with $\frac{2}{3}$ power set, it proceeds royally across the aerodrome towards the hangar. The aviator has the strong impression that he has been merely a passenger whom the aeroplane has condescended to carry, for in retrospect he is painfully aware that he has had very little control over the situation!

At last we close the throttle and switch off. The silence can be felt, and the vibrant, seemingly living craft has again become inanimate, a museum piece, a curiosity – until next time!

We leave the airfield with a deep sense of satisfaction, for we have learned a lot in that short flight, and have begun to appreciate the true meaning of the freedom of flying. We have also learned a new respect for the courage and skill of the men who first staggered shakily into the skies and pioneered heavier-than-air flight.

6 *The Avro Triplane IV*
Neil Williams

None of A. V. Roe's early triplanes has survived in airworthy condition, but a reproduction of the Mark IV Triplane was built for the film 'Those Magnificent Men in their Flying Machines' and as such it had to be sufficiently controllable and reliable to allow the scenes to be filmed safely. It speaks highly for Roe's design when one discovers that it was the best 'flyer' of all the machines used in the film.

Because the film would be seen by hawk-eyed and knowledgeable schoolboys, it was decided to incorporate the original wing-warping lateral control instead of substituting ailerons. This produced the attendant problems of the possibility of too much flexibility, resulting in flutter, which had so often resulted in disaster in the past. One of the worst forms of wing flutter is caused by the ability of the centre of pressure to move ahead of the elastic axis of the wing when the wing itself is not sufficiently rigid.

The ingenuity of the design was soon made clear when it was found that the flexural axis of the wings was, in fact, the leading edge! Lateral control was further improved by fitting hinges to the rear spars, thus allowing the wings to warp without actually bending the spars. This in turn produced lighter control forces. The term 'lighter' is used in the absolute relative sense! In 1909 the only requirement was that the machine should fly: whether it did so by immense muscular effort or sheer willpower alone was immaterial, as long as it flew. The pilot of a modern aeroplane is accustomed to built-in stability, finger-tip control, a good margin of power, almost 100% reliability, and a high degree of comfort.

Half-way across the aerodrome at a height of 50 feet in the

Triplane on my first flight, I remember thinking that I would give a month's pay to be safely back on terra firma once more. 'Why', you will ask, 'at only 50 feet up, did you not land straight ahead?' Answer: because with the throttle locked wide open and two hands on the wheel, I felt that I was only just in charge of the situation and provided the engine kept running, I might possibly, within the next half hour, learn enough about this monstrosity to attempt a landing without breaking both it and me. Certainly I did not feel confident enough to attempt a landing earlier. After about five minutes I let go of the wheel with one hand in order to throttle down the engine, a move which nearly 'upset the boat' in no mean fashion. It was another ten minutes before I could fly it one-handed. The old pioneers certainly gained my respect that day.

One has to actually sit in the machine to experience the incredible feeling of insecurity resulting from sitting in an open fuselage (as opposed to cockpit) with one's legs stretched almost full-length in order to place the feet on two tiny blocks of wood, which turn out to be the rudder pedals. A bar across the fuselage above the pilot's legs supports the elevator control and acts as a pivot for it. The control has a curious 'top dead centre' feeling, and will fall fully forward or backward when displaced from centre. The leather-covered control wheel operates wing-warping on top and centre mainplanes, and there are no stops. One continues to wind the wheel watching the wings deflect until the thought of the original 'sudden twang' causes one to desist. Finally, a glance behind completes the horrifying picture. Directly behind the tiny seat back one can look straight down at Mother Earth!

Not only that, but at the same time one of the mechanics with an evil sense of humour has given the tailplane a light shake – and the complete rear fuselage flexes! One immediately resolves that the rear portion of the aeroplane is not suitable for the eyes of sensitive and impressionable aviators, and one proceeds in the hope that, provided the front end can be managed satisfactorily, the rear end will follow. At least it always has up to now.

From this vantage point, one is treated to the spectacle of the operation of a four-stroke engine, apparently in cutaway form. On closer inspection it is discovered that the engine is actually complete, and one stares wonderingly at a neat row of rocker-

arms, valve-springs and push-rods. There being no cockpit or windscreen, one is able to watch the mechanic as he goes about his ritual of priming the engine. Incredulously I watch him produce a petrol-soaked rag and thrust it into the carburettor intake! 'Switches off, throttle closed, suck in'. The propeller is pulled over three or four compressions, and I am relieved to note that the rag is then extracted from the intake! Surprisingly the engine starts first swing, and makes a raucous clatter as the rocker-arms are galvanised into a metallic blur, sending a fine spray of oil over the unfortunate aviator. Not content with this, condensation forms on the intake manifold and is blown backwards to combine with the oil, thus providing the occupant with a greasy cold shower.

The temperature rise of the engine can be gauged by the fact that the blast of air over one's unprotected body has lost the initial chill. The chocks are waved away and the throttle advanced, the only immediate effect being a rise in the noise level and an increase in the rearward flow of oil and water. Finally about two-thirds power persuades the machine to roll reluctantly forward, after which encouragement it progresses more readily. Turning is something of a problem, and short radius turns can only be made unassisted by holding the wheel fully forward and using full rudder and a short burst of full power to lift the tail clear of the ground and swing it around. However, I recall how easily the mechanic twisted and flexed the rear fuselage and so I am content to make gentle turns only.

With the aircraft aligned into wind, the throttle is opened fully. By this time one is so impregnated with oil and water that one feels that the machine must have by this time done its worst. How wrong can one be!

The take-off is actually surprisingly easy. The machine rides extremely well on its soft, well-damped undercarriage, and although reluctant to fly, it eventually responds to a steady pull force. Once actually in the air, it settles down to the task of showing its long-suffering passenger its mettle. I use the word passenger advisedly, since one has relatively little control over the situation from this point onward. In only light turbulence one feels that control in pitch is about to be lost at any moment. As the machine hits a bump one is subjected to the usual lurch, but this is immediately followed by the horrifying sensation that the fuselage is bending as the tailplane encounters the same disturbance. So far, I have not had the courage to look!

As if this were not enough to occupy my attention, I become aware that the machine is buffeting slightly and has stopped climbing, in spite of the fact that the engine is clattering happily away, dispensing oil and water with apparent enthusiasm. Gradually the reason for the loss of performance becomes clear; with no means of measuring slip or skid it is only too easy to allow the aircraft to escape from the balanced condition, especially when flying across the wind at an inevitably low altitude. In a normal open cockpit aircraft one can assess slip or skid by the slipstream around the windscreen, but on the Triplane there is (a) no way of estimating the exact direction of the slipstream and (b) no windscreen for the slipstream to act upon. Cautiously I yaw the machine from side to side and by a process of trial and error I retrieve some of our lost performance. During these experiments I am subjected to a complete range of discomfort, with the one exception that when the machine is in balanced flight one basks in a wave of warm air from the Cirrus engine, which, incidentally, was built in 1928.

As one presses on the rudder bar in one direction one receives a blast of cold air, while in the other direction one is subjected to a shower bath. All of this is in addition to the fairly continuous lubrication process. One might imagine that by sticking labels on the toes of one's shoes marked 'WET' and 'COLD' one could perhaps patent a novel type of slip indicator, by pressing down on the foot describing the pilot's environment at any given moment!

Having mastered all of this, one may now proceed in the reasonable hope that the flight may, after all, be brought in due course to a successful conclusion. However, the appearance of some light turbulence produces some more hair-raising behaviour.

A mild wing-drop in bumpy conditions in a modern light aeroplane can be corrected with a little aileron and a touch of rudder, and would pass almost unnoticed by a passenger. The same wing-drop in the Triplane has the makings of an incipient disaster from the pilot's point-of-view as he winds the wheel with the energy of a London bus driver taking a sharp corner. All to no avail, as the wing continues to go down, and one has the horrifying impression that the whole lot is about to turn turtle like a small yacht in a gale. A bootful of rudder on its own has only one result; the nose is yawed skyward with the inevitable loss of airspeed, producing no rolling movement whatsoever. Using full 'aileron' and rudder and a fair amount of strength I hardly dare to breathe as the Triplane ponderously regains level flight. I realise that I have been treated to a basic lesson in aerodynamics, for the Triplane does not have sweepback, or stagger and the wash in/wash out of the wing changes with the use of the lateral control. Also there is hardly any keel area aft of the CG resulting in no lateral or directional stability and no interaction between rudder and 'aileron' controls. No wonder I had trouble with balanced flight!

By this time I have learned enough about the aeroplane to risk a landing, so I decide to throttle back and glide – another mistake! When the engine is throttled down or stops in a machine like the Triplane, the aircraft stops very soon afterwards, due to the very high drag and low density of the structure. Most of the time in flight is spent at full throttle with the engine valiantly trying to overcome the colossal drag. Quickly I depress the bows of the machine, but quick as I am, the speed has still dropped to 30 knots from the normal cruising speed of 45 knots.

As the aircraft settles into the glide the warm air from the engine can be felt moving upwards across one's body until at 30 knots I am subjected to a stream of cold air from the vicinity of the undercarriage. At the same time I notice smoke from the exhaust curling up all over the wing. The aircraft is still flying well, but the rate of sink is alarmingly high. I try setting half throttle and with the speed increased to 40 knots the machine is under control. Now we are over the grass, no more than ten feet up. Slowly I ease back on the throttle, lowering the aircraft cautiously, until suddenly the machine sinks quickly. I pull back on the wheel, and as the tail comes down we cut the throttle. Instantly we are on the ground, with a ridiculously short landing roll. I realise that the sink at the last moment is due to downwash over the tail being influenced by ground effect. I taxy back to the hangars, greatly relieved to have completed the flight without mishap, but such is the magic and thrill of flying the machine that I am already looking forward to flying it again. Old in design and delicate it may be, but it is much more demanding to fly than any modern aeroplane, and there is a tremendous sense of satisfaction to be derived from flying it properly. It can be both a salutory and rewarding experience, demanding a high degree of attention and skill from even the most highly qualified pilots of the Shuttleworth Collection.

7 *The Blackburn*

Neil Williams

With the increase in the popularity of the range of Blackburn types in 1912, a new monoplane was commissioned with the intention of giving exhibitions of flying – perhaps the first custom-built display aircraft? This machine was delivered in 1913 and after giving several exhibitions at Leeds it changed hands and flew to its new home at Wittering, Lincs, where it was crashed soon afterwards. There it remained, broken and desolate, for some twenty-five years, when by a happy chance it was acquired by the Shuttleworth Collection and rebuilt to its original state.

After the end of the Second World War the Collection's aircraft appeared at many flying displays and, from 1966, at the Collection's Open Days at Old Warden, but the Blackburn, together with the slightly earlier Bleriot and Deperdussin, were relegated to low straight hops across the airfield.

With its flying career seemingly drawing to a close, interest waned, particularly with the advent of the replicas like the Boxkite and Triplane, which could entertain the crowds more spectacularly. While the pilots at Old Warden were certainly interested to 'hop' the veterans, because no test pilot is able to resist flying something different, even for a few seconds, there is a world of difference between 'hopping' and making a full circuit.

So it was that when I was asked to 'hop' the Blackburn my primary concern was not to see if I could get as high as possible for as long as I could, but rather to ensure that I did not damage the oldest aeroplane in the Collection capable of real flight. It is a very different sensation climbing into a real veteran rather than a replica; one feels an ENORMOUS responsibility. One is aware of the attention of the mechanics who have spent long hours restoring this old aeroplane; they will not make adverse comment but one cannot help feeling that this machine really belongs to them. One becomes intensely self-critical; any fumbling, any unnecessary bursts of power, can produce a high degree of self-recrimination.

There is no such thing as a quick familiarisation 'hop', with precious engine hours guarded so devotedly. Ineed, one is lucky to have the opportunity to run the engine at all before the display, so one hopes the crowd will be sympathetic towards any pilot who stops his engine in mid-field – rotary engine life is measured in minutes! The immediate problem I encountered was rather fundamental – how did I get in? Before I could phrase the question, a short wooden ladder appeared miraculously from nowhere. (Later I learned that it had been borrowed from the Boxkite.) However, I consoled myself with the thought that there were plenty of natural footholds for an athletic pilot on that aeroplane.

I arrived at the cockpit area only to find that a solid-looking fuselage cross-member effectively prevented my getting into the pilot's chair. To my horror one of the mechanics gave it a sharp tug, whereupon it hinged upwards, allowing access to the seat. Once seated, with the cross-member clipped down, it acts as a safety bar, almost dispensing with the need to use the harness. However, being a firm believer in both belt and braces, I secured the Sutton harness. The geometry of the cockpit leaves much to be desired, as the pedals are too far away and are very close together, while the wheel, closely resembling the steering wheel of a sports car in both shape and location, moves in a completely foreign manner. Instead of moving in a fore-and-aft plane, the control column is attached to a pivot beneath the panel, with the result that when the elevators are up the wheel swings downwards until it practically touches the seat, while with full down elevator the wheel moves up until it obliterates all forward view. This vertical motion of the wheel takes quite a bit of getting used to. Ailerons of course are non-existent, but it is fascinating to operate the wing-warping and to see the large chord wing twisting with the able assistance of a conglomeration of pulleys and cables.

The instrument panel is painfully simple. There, in the centre, in solitary splendour, reposes a rev counter. That is it.

No ASI, altimeter, or even oil pressure gauge, the latter, I suppose, being a bit superfluous on a rotary engine anyway, as the aviator can be in no doubt that oil is being supplied to the engine, if he is to judge by the amount of castor oil that usually drenches him. There is no windscreen, and the pilot sits practically on, rather than in the fuselage, thus requiring warm and oil-proof clothing even on a summer's day. Although the Blackburn is rather spartan in its accessories it is at least liberally endowed with engine controls: there are five of them! There they sit, practically defying the aviator to find the right combination for starting. A large brass Victorian electric light switch has been pressed into service as a magneto switch, and there is an ignition cutout (blip) button on the wheel. This latter can dispense some painful electric shocks to keep the aviator on his toes!

At first glance one is horrified to see what appear to be no fewer than three throttle levers, but a reassuring explanation is soon forthcoming. There is indeed a throttle, which works in theory only; subsequent experiment showed that although it did operate after a fashion, it also flooded the engine at low revs. The other two controls were the standard rotary engine air lever and fine adjustment lever. All of this for a seven-cylinder 50 hp engine.

Having satisfied myself that I was securely installed and that the primitive control system was likely to function to order, I passed the few minutes before starting in absorbing the appearance and attitude of the machine as it sat on the ground, for with no flight instruments this exercise was to be carried out literally by the seat of the pants. In spite of my preoccupation I was able from my vantage point to observe the staggering flight of the other two veterans with their tiny three-cylinder engines, and was pleased to note that they were not being affected by that terrible meteorological phenomenon, light turbulence. Even the Bleriot managed a hop of 50 yards. Now the Gnome was being primed, with neat petrol being injected into each tiny cylinder. I set the engine controls according to the briefing: throttle near full, air lever set to half and petrol (fine adjustment) closed. The Gnome was pulled over with that wheezing clonk peculiar to rotaries, and an invisible prop swinger shouted 'contact'. The Victorian brass switch was selected on, and the prop was swung. The little engine instantly roared into life in a cloud of blue castor oil smoke as the priming fuel caught. I waited until this was exhausted, and when the engine cut out, I opened the fine adjustment, whereupon the Gnome picked up again and buzzed away merrily. Thirty seconds after starting and the engine was ready for take-off, for this is a dead loss oil system. I occupied this time by finding the positions of air lever and fine adjustment for full power and slow running, the only two realistic settings on a rotary engine. Full power gives a clean 1,200 rpm, and it idles at 700 to 800.

I waved the chocks away and used the button to blip the engine as I taxied the few yards to the take-off point. I was concerned in case even in this short time the plugs might oil up, but the Gnome ran sweetly, just like a sewing machine. Two burly mechanics held the tail as I increased power to maximum, and as I dropped my hand they released their grip. The monoplane ran lightly across the grass, as I dabbed the rudder experimentally. It didn't seem to make much difference, so I left it alone. The aircraft ignored me completely and continued to run straight. I wondered how fast I was going – it looked about fast enough to fly. I thought the tail was up but I couldn't be really sure – the confused slip-stream with no windscreen ahead of me had destroyed my sense of feel. I tugged experimentally at the wheel – I couldn't move it! What was happening? I pulled even harder, with no result, then I remembered the wheel must come down for the elevators to go up. I tried this gently, and momentarily we were airborne; with no ASI I was afraid of stalling and as I relaxed the pressure she sank back to earth. At least she was stable. I repeated the experiment, and this time I noted she responded slowly to the lateral control. But now we were running out of field; the engine levers required me to stretch forward to reach them, so rather than unbalance the craft I held down the blip button, receiving a series of painful electric shocks in the process! The Blackburn sank gently to the ground, and at last I was able to reach the levers and release the confounded button. What a way to fly! I was covered with castor oil and my hand was still tingling. But for several seconds it really flew. There was no wind so I had the machine turned around for the return hop. This time I held her just clear of the ground and found that she responded gently but correctly to the controls, but I was still having trouble with the elevator control system. But somehow, though she had not exceeded ten feet of altitude for many years, I had the feeling that she had enough thrust and control to really fly.

I waited impatiently for the end of the display before approaching David Ogilvy, Shuttleworth's General Manager, with the idea: what an added attraction it would be if this old aeroplane could demonstrate FULL flight. David at first hesitated but then agreed that if the machine made two more hops and did not falter, then I could take responsibility for the aircraft during a circuit. I knew what that meant if anything went wrong. The engine again hummed sweetly as though eager to carry the machine into the air. The two hops were uneventful, except that I used every second to gain as much knowledge of the aeroplane as I could. Again the mechanics held me back as I carefully set the engine to full power, trying to listen for any change in note that might herald trouble, and sensitive to any possible vibration. 1,200 rpm, healthy and steady, and as I again dropped my hand, the tail was released. Straight and true she rolled, accelerating gently, but this time, hopefully, she would not be made to stop. The engine beat strongly as we passed the point where she unstuck on the last run, but I let her roll, gathering speed, for I was afraid of getting on the wrong side of the drag curve. I pressed gently down on the wheel and she lifted off cleanly. For a few seconds I held her parallel to the ground, noting carefully the nose position on the horizon, then I let her settle into the gentlest of climbs with the nose cowling apparently one inch above the horizon. The engine was as smooth as a turbine at 1,220 rpm, and I decided that if I maintained this rpm, with a healthy engine, I must have reached the optimum condition for climbing. I was two-thirds down the field at about 30 feet. Now was the time to stop – or never. The machine was willing – now we were committed, but as I left the field behind me she was starting to sink; with mounting alarm I flew as carefully as I knew how, coaxing her, giving a little, taking a little. Down, down, now we were only ten feet over the standing corn, the engine still pulling with all of its tiny heart. And slowly, very slowly, again we started to climb.

Now there was a new hazard – telephone wires ahead! I flew directly at them, with one eye on the rev counter – 1,240 rpm;

that must mean excess speed above normal climb speed. I lifted her over the wires, and dived a little to regain speed. There was open countryside ahead, and I concentrated on gaining height before trying a turn back to the field. I knew that everyone on the field was deeply concerned, but I placed my trust in that sturdy little engine and kept climbing. Now for a turn – to the right would be best. I was 200 or 300 feet up, so I could afford to lower the nose a little. The flat Bedfordshire countryside rotated steadily beyond the round aluminium cowling, and at last I was heading back towards the field. But now something else was wrong – the aircraft was shuddering – surely it couldn't be stalling? I lowered the nose, the shuddering got worse; what on earth was happening? Then I remembered my experiences with the Triplane, which behaved in the same way when the controls were crossed. I checked – the rudder seemed more or less central, but I just could not tell by looking whether I was carrying any wing-warp. The left wing felt heavy so I pressed gentle right rudder. The shuddering disappeared and so did the wing heaviness. With such an exposed cockpit I just could not tell if I was side-slipping. Everything was slowly getting blurred as the castor oil spray settled on my goggles. In my struggles to get a handkerchief out of my pocket the machine reared up and I instinctively pushed on the wheel. Of course, nothing happened for long seconds until I remembered that I must lift the wheel to lower the nose. It was only five minutes since I took off, but it seemed like an hour. Everything was now running with castor oil, and I was sure that the oil deflector was not fitted when the machine was rebuilt. As I reached the field I estimated my height at 700 feet, every inch a struggle against drag and gravity. Now the monoplane seemed to have remembered how to fly, for I was not working so hard, and the turns were more co-ordinated. She curved gracefully in the sky, almost transparent with her clear-doped fabric showing her skeletal construction. So frail she looked from the ground, but high above the earth she felt a sturdy little machine, willing and responsive. I was amazed at her docility and gentle stability; was this a design of accident, or the product of a brilliant mind?

The light was going; we had to go down.

I pulled back the fine adjustment and we glided easily in a gentle spiral; the nose was well down, and I had changed my grip on the wheel. By holding it with both hands together at the top I could control the machine with a normal push-pull action. As we came in over the woods in a steep controlled glide I realised with a little surprise that I had not consciously been concerned by the absence of an airspeed indicator. Somehow she felt right, and somehow I knew that this was the right speed, without knowing what it actually was. With the fine adjustment closed, I let her settle and she touched delicately on three points as lightly as a feather; what a delightful old aeroplane! I caught the engine on the fine adjustment and taxied on the button, receiving another shock from the infernal thing.

Now the old Blackburn has entered another era of her experience, for, weather permitting, she will be able to fly properly on flying days, a wonderful historical exhibit, showing not only the achievement of a pioneer, but by comparison, the achievement of the intervening years.

8 *The Avro 504K*
Air Commodore A. H. Wheeler

The Avro 504K was the standard primary trainer for the Royal Flying Corps and later the Royal Air Force for approximately 12 years from 1915 to 1927; even in 1927 there was only a change of engine to the Armstrong Siddeley Lynx radial which made it an Avro 504N. The early history of the Collection's specimen is unknown, but it was acquired from the de Havilland Aircraft Co. and was restored by the apprentices of Messrs. A. V. Roe and Company. It was a Lynx-engined 504N, converted to K standard during restoration.

The 504K was a fairly easy aeroplane to fly by standards obtaining in those days, but of course nothing like as easy as the modern light aeroplane with a tricycle undercarriage and a docile engine. To start off with the Avro has a very definite tendency to swing during take-off and the balanced rudder (with no fin) is light and effective making it all too easy for beginners to overcorrect a swing. Instructors in those early days usually left take-off instruction till late in the training schedule. In the air flying fairly straight and fairly level the Avro behaves well but it is very ready to deviate from the straight and level on any provocation at all. Once one has mastered the control responses and trained one's reflexes to act instinctively, restoring lateral deviations from the straight and level is easy since the ailerons are not unduly sensitive and the large span of the Avro renders the rolling movement fairly sluggish. Even the most ham-handed pilot therefore has plenty of time to ease off the aileron force as the Avro comes laterally level.

The rudder and, to a lesser extent, the elevator require more careful treatment. Both are very sensitive with the engine on but ease off in sensitivity to a significant extent when the engine is not on power. Since the rotary engine (see chapter 3 on handling a rotary) is essentially either on full power or completely shut off, with virtually no intermediary power setting at all, the change in effectiveness of the rudder and elevator can be very abrupt. This affects the actions to be taken on engine failure particularly near the stall.

The Avro 504K is very light with a lot of built-in drag: therefore there is very little time for a pilot to pick up gliding speed, and gliding angle, when the engine is stopped – either intentionally or unintentionally. Action therefore has to be very quick indeed if the engine fails on take-off. One does not look around to pick a suitable landing area for that has, within close limits, already been determined; one merely pushes the stick forward till a steep angle of glide is achieved then, and only then, does one look for a landing area, perhaps with only a couple of hundred feet of height to spare giving a maximum gliding distance of about 300 yards, according to wind strength.

If the pilot does not take this immediate action on engine failure the Avro will stall within seconds and at least half a turn of a spin will probably result with a loss of height of about 150 feet, leaving no choice at all for a landing and probably having turned out of wind in the half turn of the spin.

Stalling and spinning on the Avro is a relatively sluggish affair by the standards of many light aeroplanes of its date. It falls into a stall or spin, it does not flick into them but if this happens below 500 feet recovery action must be taken quickly – stick forward and opposite rudder – the Avro then comes out immediately. It is for this reason that the aerobatic manoeuvre, the 'falling leaf' can be done so effectively by holding the stick back and applying opposite rudder, as the Avro comes out of one incipient spin and is ready to fall into another the other way as the wings momentarily come level.

The reason for describing the stalling characteristics of the Avro early on and in detail is that this is the only feature wherein the Avro differs markedly from modern light aeroplanes – apart from the rotary engine.

Having mastered the engine handling the pilot can taxy across wind or down wind so long as wind speeds do not exceed about 7 knots. Above that speed it is advisable to have wing tip men bearing in mind the Avro has no brakes and only an unsteerable tail-skid to slow it down. Without wing tip men and in light winds it is possible to control the Avro on the ground very effectively giving bursts of engine with 'stick' forward, when corrections are required. The ailerons are of significant assistance in taxying due to their drag, particularly down wind, when the wind (behind) acts on the down-going aileron pushing it forward: into wind the opposite aileron is used so that the wind acts on the down-going aileron pushing it back. This is a taxying technique which has largely been forgotten with modern aeroplanes having brakes and steerable nose or tail wheels.

Except for the tendency to swing particularly when the tail-skid is lifted off the ground the take-off is perfectly straightforward and, in light winds can be made across wind if necessary. In such cases it is advisable to depress the wing on the windward side so that no drift occurs when ground bumps and the bungee undercarriage combine to throw the Avro into the air before it is ready to fly. The undercarriage will stand a certain amount of side loads due to drift but it is as well not to overtax it.

Take-off speed should be at about 35 mph (30 knots) to allow for gusts and not to overstrain the undercarriage by running fast over uneven ground. All tail-skid aeroplanes without brakes, like the Avro, are relatively uncontrollable on a runway, particularly at the end of a landing run, so a grass surface is always preferable – particularly for landing.

A good climbing speed is anywhere between 45 and 50 mph (40-44 knots) but the higher speed is preferable since it allows a little more time to pick up gliding speed if the engine should fail. Having mastered the take-off there are no problems about ordinary level flight. The Avro is unstable in the practical sense in that it wanders off its course if not corrected continually but it does it so sluggishly that it is no embarrassment: in fact, that was one of the characteristics that made it such a good trainer – a pupil could not relax for long. The most noticeable feature of the Avro which distinguishes it from more modern aeroplanes is the strong aileron drag effect caused by the down-going aileron with a corresponding reduction of drag on the up-going aileron: the result of this is that if one banks the Avro to turn one way without significant rudder to counteract

the drag the Avro banks the way intended but turns fairly quickly in the other direction. This was a characteristic which was present in all aeroplanes of that date and indeed up till about 1930 in decreasing degree according to whether the designer used the later sophisticated design of ailerons or used the older type.

Much has been said and written about the gyroscopic effect of the rotary engine on the handling of aeroplanes and on such small aeroplanes as the Camel or the Snipe with large and powerful rotary engines installed the effect was very marked. On the Snipe one could only just hold the nose above the horizon with full left rudder in a steep right hand turn and all elevator movements produced a secondary 'kick' from the engines gyroscopic response. This is, however, not at all marked in the Avro 504K. One can notice the gyroscopic response in a steep turn but it is not seriously embarrassing and there is no question of running out of left rudder in a steep right hand turn.

Landing the Avro 504K presents no real problem for an experienced pilot but for a beginner two factors make it rather a worry. Firstly the resilience in the undercarriage is provided by 'bungee' rubber cord which has virtually no damping effect: it therefore gives back all it gets and with pilots unable to judge height precisely it gets quite a lot. The result of misjudging the landing height and dropping the Avro from (say) 10 inches is a rebound into the air followed by another drop and a further rebound which can continue across the aerodrome almost until the end of the landing run. With the rotary engine one cannot soften the subsequent bounces by gentle application of engine power since the rotary engine is shut off for landing: to use the engine at all one has to open the petrol control lever again or release the blip switch according to which technique is used in engine control (see chapter on rotary engine control) and then the engine gives a full throttle roar which is all right for going round again but a bit unmanageable if needed for smoothing out a bouncy landing. With a rotary engine the approved method of approach and landing was, and still is, to arrive at a suitable position down wind of the aerodrome and at an altitude of about 500 feet and then switch off the engine by pulling back the fine adjustment (petrol supply) lever; after that one approaches the aerodrome in a series of gliding turns followed by a nicely judged side-slip as one comes over the aerodrome boundary. At this stage one can give the engine a burst of power so as to clear it and spin it up ready for 'catching' it after landing. One then eases out of the very steep approach angle so as to be flying almost level at 20 feet, i.e. when one can recognise grass as individual blades and not just a green mass; one then loses the last 20 feet and excess speed (about 15 mph) as one approaches the ground. If one judges this correctly the wheels and the tail skid will touch at the same time. As soon as one is firmly on the ground one pushes the petrol lever forward and 'catches' the engine as it opens up with a roar, one 'blips' it with the ignition (blip) switch and eases the petrol lever back till the engine adopts a sort of rough idling speed running in the 'dot-and-go-one' manner associated with rotary engines. At this engine setting and with an occasional 'blip' on the ignition switch one can taxy in, but beginners usually tend to use the 'blip' switch excessively being unable to adjust the petrol lever correctly.

With the engine shut off completely and the nose pulled up till the Avro stalls, a spin can be entered in either direction by application of rudder in the appropriate direction. The spin is relatively slow and recovery is immediate by normal methods, i.e. opposite rudder and forward (or centralised) elevator. Loss of height during recovery is about 150-200 feet before level flight is attained.

In stalling, spinning and the falling leaf manoeuvre there is a possibility that the engine (and propeller) will stop turning. This may be a cause for concern by pilots new to the rotary but so long as one has sufficient height a dive up to about 100 mph (88 knots) will usually be sufficient to get the engine over the first compression and start it turning again. Getting over the first compression can be assisted by a sudden application of aileron – in the right direction.

A loop in the Avro is a perfectly straightforward manoeuvre entered by diving to between 90 and 100 mph (80-88 knots) and then pulling firmly up and over keeping straight with significant rudder control. At the top of the loop the speed will drop to about 45 mph (40 knots) but will pick up again quickly in the ensuing dive. As speed builds up the engine should be shut off completely by closing the fuel lever in order to prevent overspeeding, and only opened again on reaching level flight, probably with a speed of about 80 mph (70 knots). If a second loop is intended immediately following the first the engine can be put on power a little earlier.

Due to sluggish aileron control a roll off the top of a loop is virtually impossible or if achieved is a very untidy manoeuvre.

A barrel roll, i.e. a loop pulled out sideways is possible but not a very effective display manoeuvre because so little assistance can be got from the ailerons. For the same reason – ineffective aileron control – a slow roll is virtually impossible to perform in any way which would make it a recognisable manoeuvre and if attempted would impose a strain on the rigging which is best avoided.

The stall turn which, when developed more dramatically, was sometimes called the 'Immelmann' turn is an easy manoeuvre for the Avro since the pilot merely pulls the nose up till the Avro is climbing almost vertically, kicks on full rudder to turn in whichever direction is required and lets the Avro fall over that way closing the fuel level as it enters the ensuing dive. Very little height need be lost in this manoeuvre.

Closely allied to this manoeuvre is the half roll which in its tamest form in the Avro can be indulged in – by experienced pilots – on the early stages of an approach for landing.

The side slip is a most useful manoeuvre on the landing approach for losing excess height and speed. For this the nose is pulled up slightly above the horizon, full aileron is applied with the necessary rudder control to hold the nose up and the Avro slips sideways towards the ground with greatly increased drag from the fuselage which prevents a build up of speed.

To sum up, briefly, the flying characteristics of the Avro 504K one may say it is a very easy aeroplane to fly if one treats it with reasonable respect. If an experienced pilot learns how to handle the engine he can fly the aeroplane.

9 The Sopwith Pup

John Lewis

The Sopwith Pup was a fighter aircraft of the first World War, at a time when such aircraft were known as scouts. It was developed from the Sopwith $1\frac{1}{2}$ Strutter, and was ordered for the RNAS in 1916. Later, it was also supplied to the RFC, with which it became a standard equipment and earned the reputation of being a first class flying machine. With the RNAS it played a major role in the development of carrier ship-borne aircraft operation. Although its official name was the Sopwith Scout, Pup is the name by which it was always known, and by which it became famous.

The collection Pup, N5180, was the property of a private owner near Bedford until it was acquired by Richard Shuttleworth in 1936. It was in fact then a Dove, a two seat variant of the Pup, and had to be re-converted back to its original form by the Collection. Since then it has appeared regularly in displays throughout the country in the form it is seen today. The motor is an 80 hp le Rhone 9 cylinder rotary, in which the crankshaft is fixed to the aircraft, and the cylinders rotate, together with the propeller, which is fixed to the crankcase. Since most of the problems, and hence the interest, of aircraft fitted with rotary motors arises from the unique operation of such power plants, considerable time will be spent in this article in exploring the topic, as well as looking at the aeroplane itself.

The aircraft is a wholly conventional wire and strut braced biplane, typical of its era. It is fabric covered throughout, and has the normal modern control set-up of ailerons, elevators and rudder. In order to improve the available rate of roll, an important consideration in fighter aircraft, the ailerons are doubled, a set being fitted to both upper and lower mainplanes. The undercarriage has bungee sprung wire mainwheels set close together, and has no damping; and a swivelling tail-skid of a rather unyielding nature. Bamboo hoops are mounted beneath the wing tips of the lower mainplanes to protect them in the event of roll angle developing on the ground. A single Vickers machine gun is fitted between the centre section struts, with a heavy glass windshield mounted on the butt end near to the pilot. A synchronising gear enabled this gun to fire safely through the propeller.

The cockpit is extremely roomy, but the fixed basket seat is rather hard and uncomfortable, and the tall pilot projects a long way out into the airflow. The rudder pedals, too, are a rather long way from the seat, and the pilot is restrained by a very uncomfortable and inefficient set of straps. The field of view is good, except where obscured by the upper wing, but the suspicion dawns that the windshield is not going to be a lot of use. There is a gap between it and the fuselage upper decking, and it is extremely small. On the right is a hand pump for raising pressure in the fuselage tank, and near it a valve to adjust the blow-off pressure of the safety valve. The instruments are few, consisting of an ASI, altimeter, slip bubble, RPM indicator, oil flow glass, compass and pressure gauge for the tank. On the left hand wall are the most important controls in a rotary powered aircraft, the air and fuel levers and magneto switch. A further ignition cut-out button is fitted onto the top of the conventional spade grip control column, to enable power reductions to be made by 'blipping' the ignition circuit.

The motor is unusual in that it has only one push rod per barrel, and this operates both inlet and exhaust valves, pushing for one and pulling for the other. This was done in the interests of lightness and low centrifugal loading. Ignition is by single magneto, and the oil system is, of course, total loss. The big end system is extremely unusual in that there is no master rod as in most other radial and rotary powerplants, but the different length rods are equipped with a most ingenious system of shoes which fit into matching grooves at the big end, and which provide rotation without interference. Displacement at nearly eleven litres is large, but the fuel consumption is modest, and the motor extremely smooth when running.

More than one pilot, returning stunned from his first flight in a rotary powered aircraft, when asked what he thought of the aircraft, has said 'How would I know? – I spent all my time worrying about the motor. I didn't even notice the aircraft.' I have to admit that I myself had just the same reaction, and since subsequent flights showed that the aircraft was indeed quite normal and unexceptionable, the major content of this article is going to have to be rotary handling, with a little about the aircraft thrown in, rather than the more normal reverse. Indeed, in view of the general awkwardness and unhandy behaviour of the rotary, it is a wonder that anyone learned to fly at all in even relative safety in the days when they were the rule. The reader might like to dwell on this as he reads on and the description develops, and contrast it with what he knows of the simplicity of modern powerplant handling.

The pre-flight walk-round inspection is normal and is confined to the normal aspects of airframe condition, rigging tension, security of panels, tyre pressure and so on. A single footstep cut into the fuselage near the trailing edge of the lower wing enables a rather undignified scramble into the cockpit to be made. Having sat down it is normal to find that either the cushion is the wrong thickness, or that one is sitting on the straps, and so one usually stands right up again. Once these matters are sorted out, however, strapping in is rapidly completed, the controls checked for freedom and correct sense, and the magneto, fuel and air all confirmed off. Pressure is then pumped up in the tank, and the pressure blow-off checked at $2\frac{1}{2}$ psi and adjusted if necessary. The big rotary is now liberally primed into each cylinder with a syringe and pulled over a couple of times, to suck in the mixture. This priming stage is very important, and is one of the secrets of a good start on this type of motor. The skill of the engineer in knowing just how much to give is everything. The air and fuel levers are marked with numbered calibrations for reference, and have a friction device for locking them into the selected position. The air lever is first set open by the amount thought appropriate for the day, say halfway for a cold, dense day, rather less for a hot one, and the fuel re-checked off. This last is vital – too much fuel during a start guarantees failure. Then, with the mag switch on, the engineer swings the prop smartly over a couple of compressions. If the prime was right, and the motor cold – they are

very awkward when half hot – it will fire at once, and with a cloud of smoke and a blast of air from the propeller, burst up to its maximum of about 1,150 rpm, rocking the aircraft wildly on its narrow undercarriage as the torque reaction sets it. It is now extremely important to have patience; a rotary can very easily be made too rich, and if this occurs it will stop, and have to be blown out before it can once again be started. The pilot waits, therefore, until the prime is exhausted, and the motor cuts and starts to run down. As it does this he applies fuel, using the lever on the left, while at the same time ensuring that he does not alter the air setting, to a point at which experience or a briefing tells him the motor will run. If he has got it right, after a couple of seconds delay, normal for the rotary as the mixture finds its way through to the cylinders, the motor will pick up again and all is well. It is then a matter of experiment to alter the settings of air and fuel levers in sequence repeatedly until the motor runs smoothly at the maximum obtainable rpm. This will vary from day to day, but in any case should be better than 1,100. The settings of air and fuel are then noted and committed to memory for the subsequent flight.

Reducing power on a rotary can only be done to a limited extent using fuel, usually down to about 750 rpm. At this setting power is excessive still for taxying, so further reduction must be done by cutting the ignition. This is possible using the mag switch, but it is far more convenient to do it by depressing the button on the stick with the right thumb. There is a knack to doing this, rather akin to patting your head and rubbing your tummy at the same time. Try that, then try to hold a conversation with someone at the same time, but don't break the sequence. Not easy, is it? In fact, like everything, it comes with practice, but in the early stages it is awfully easy to get confused. At 750 rpm the motor runs rather erratically, and sounds rather like a many cylindered two stroke, but each time the cut-out is released and it picks up, it fires steadily for a few moments, and the aircraft rocks gently on its gear. Despite the apparent approach of disaster each time the motor is allowed to run down, this condition is entirely reliable; and, possibly because the motor is running lean, plug oiling is not usually a problem.

It is at this stage that the chocks can safely be waved away, and with a handler on each wing the aircraft is taxyed away towards take-off. During the taxy the handlers work hard to keep the aircraft going towards the marshalling point, and especially so if there is any wind, as the aircraft has a will of its own on gradients and in side winds. Should the motor misbehave at this stage, the handlers will also have to hold it back whilst the pilot opens up a little, clears the plugs and resets the mixture to a more reliable level. Handlers on a rotary work hard and almost need a sixth sense to help them to know what is going on. A thoughtless pilot can cause them considerable anguish, and 'have a thought for the wing men' is part of every new pilot's briefing on a rotary.

Lined up for take-off, exactly into wind as crosswind handling is very poor, the only check really necessary is that the fuel pressure is correct. If not, it is pumped up again to the required pressure with the hand pump. Usually, the prop wash will have helped the little windmill pump on the port centre section strut to maintain it, and not much pumping will be necessary. An assessment of oiling will have been possible before now due to the smell and blue smoke, but the glass is rechecked just in case, the handlers signalled clear and the fuel lever set in the full power position. The aircraft rocks again, swings a little, and gathers way extremely quickly as the power comes in. Now is the time to check rpm, and very slightly to reduce fuel setting as it comes up to the static value. This is extremely important as the rotary feeds mixture by centrifugal force and the increased rpm resulting from forward speed will lead to overrichness if this is not done. Slight overrichness will give a marked loss of power; more than slight and the motor will stop. A rotary that has had a rich cut cannot be started in the air again, except during a long descent. In fact, the ear turns out to be, as it so often is, a reliable guide to the state of the motor. The beginnings of the overrich condition are evident in a slightly heavy, flat exhaust note, and action can be taken in this as well as by watching for rpm reductions.

In any event, the aircraft accelerates so quickly that the ground break arrives before the pilot is really ready for it, and although it is normal to lift the tail first this really makes very little difference to the take-off performance. The rate and angle of climb are exceedingly brisk, and the motor smooth and crisp sounding. The blast of air past the pilot is incredible, however, and it has just enough upward component to take the breath away, and unless they are fastened like a tourniquet, the pilot's goggles too. Everyone who meets this tries the obvious dodge of ducking down into the cockpit for relief, but it is no use, the icy blast is in there too. Nothing else for it but to put up with it and to make a note to tighten the goggles for the next sortie. Those of you who have seen the Pup at displays with the pilot's hand to his head may have wondered why. Now you know – he is neither puzzled nor waving at the spectators – he is trying hard to hold his goggles onto his face so that he may contrive to see, and so to have some influence on the remainder of the flight.

In the climb the strong helical airflow from the big efficient propeller is evident from the marked rudder deflection needed, and the gyroscopic effect of the motor is powerfully evident if turns are made. Go one way and the nose drops, the other and it rises. The higher the turn rate used, the worse this becomes. It must have been the very devil of a nuisance in a fight. The ailerons and elevators are powerful and precise, however, and all the controls are very pleasantly light. No wonder the machine had such a fine reputation. For some reason, possibly connected with its reconversion, our Pup is rather tail heavy, and needs a constant push force on the control column to hold it in any flight condition. This naturally worsens as speed rises, and spoils what would otherwise be a very nice handling aeroplane.

At speed, adverse yaw from large aileron inputs is modest, and the usual trick of leading slightly with rudder controls it easily. Damping is good, and manoeuvrability superb. The point to watch in this regime is again the motor, because as speed rises so does rpm, and this rapidly approaches the limit. Exceeding this could easily lead to structural damage, so rpm must be controlled by reducing fuel or by cutting the ignition. Speed sufficient for a loop, the only aerobatic manoeuvre we permit ourselves, is obtained just about at the limit, however, both of rpm and the pilot's ability to retain his goggles, so we can usually get by without this expedient in a display, except for effect during low flypasts. It is in the low-speed regimes such as the top of the loop that the full measure of the gyro reaction is felt, and it takes real skill to do one exactly straight. At the other extreme it is easy to perform a perfect clover leaf in the Pup just by doing 4 loops in a row and by taking no opposing action at the top. It is quite uncanny to watch the aeroplane turn sedately through 90° to its original heading without any action by the pilot.

Possibly the most awkward part of the flight in the Pup is the approach and landing. This is not, again, the fault of the aircraft, but of the complication of rotary handling. The aeroplane is a very good glider, and reducing power to the 750 rpm tickover will only result in a modest descent rate insufficient for the purpose. Resort to 'blipping' is therefore made as well, and control of glideslope is thereafter fairly easy, the increased rate of descent being, literally, switched on and off as required. The disturbances to directional and lateral trim caused by this are unsettling, however, and the workload required to keep the approach tidy is considerable. The landing itself is not difficult, but to do it properly and to control the motor is. The aircraft is easy to flare, being well damped even at low speed, but once in ground effect it is necessary to kill the motor completely using the button on the stick, or the Pup will go on flying for ever, one foot off the ground. The problem lies in doing the killing for long enough to get onto the ground, without doing it for so long that the motor stops, and at the same time fly into a three point stalled landing on an aircraft with a crisply sprung and rather unforgiving undercarriage. It is not difficult to do either, but both at once is something else again. With no brakes, a narrow track and a fair tendency to roll with sideslip, the aircraft is also always landed exactly with wind, but gusts occur and sometimes directional control becomes very bad. At such a time a burst of power is needed, because once the tail is down the fin and rudder are blanked, and although effective are very weak. Fortunately, tail skid drag helps, especially if the stick is held hard back, and the landing rollout, provided too much power is not used, is usually quite short. Hopefully, the motor is still running, and careful adjustment of it at its lowest setting can now be made as the handlers approach. Since it is now very hot, greater care than before is necessary to keep from losing it as the aircraft taxies in, and it may well prove necessary to stop and reset on the way back.

I hope you have enjoyed this brief description of the problems of operating the Sopwith Pup. It is a fascinating aeroplane, all the more so for being a representative of one of the most successful aeroplanes of its age. Perhaps too, you can now see why so few modern pilots notice anything about the aeroplane on their first acquaintance with it, and you can wonder, with me, how anyone ever succeeded in teaching himself to fly successfully in an aeroplane powered by such a motor.

10   The Bristol Fighter
Wing Commander R. F. Martin

In the course of the past twenty five years, I have been lucky enough to have flown most of the aeroplanes in the Shuttleworth Collection. All of them of course are interesting, as they give an insight into the ways that past generations of designers and pilots evolved the handling qualities and performance of the aircraft of their time and the criteria by which they judged them. However, if the truth were told, there is not all that much *fun* attached to flying some of the very earliest aeroplanes. Satisfaction – certainly. But one is usually far too concerned in not hazarding an irreplaceable piece of history to extract much enjoyment from the proceedings, bearing in mind the limited controllability and susceptability to weather conditions of veteran aeroplanes.

Because it is free of so many of these anxieties and preoccupations the Bristol Fighter is, perhaps, the aircraft in the Collection for which I have the most affection. It was also, in the days when I first flew for Shuttleworth, the only aeroplane in which we flew cross-country to air displays. Like 'Peanuts', one was able to imagine oneself the World War I fighter pilot on leave from the Western Front, map reading one's way up the country to shoot a line to the locals.

My first cross-country, and indeed first flight in the Bristol Fighter, was from Old Warden to Newcastle (in 1952) with 'Jacko'* in the rear cockpit.

Now the cockpit is pretty basic. Throttle, mixture control, and hung below the quadrant, an advance and retard lever. On the right cockpit side the elevator trim. Most of the other items are concerned with the fuel system. There are two fuel tanks, on one of which one sits; the other is further forward, behind the

engine. There is a tank selector cock mounted on the left below the instrument panel which is somewhat obscurely marked, and on the right hand instrument panel a complex of brass pipes and taps controlling the pressurisation of the fuel system. A priming pump and hand operated pressure pump complete the system.

We set course from Old Warden to Sherburn-in-Elmet, where we planned to 'tech stop' and refuel, but over Leicester I changed tanks and the engine stopped. As I still had fuel in the tank on which we had been running, I switched back again and the engine picked up, but then followed a lunatic discussion of the problem with the 'Flight Engineer'. In order to make his views known, 'Jacko' practically climbed into the front cockpit and without warning wrenched up the side of my helmet and bellowed into my right ear. To prevent myself being deafened I closed the throttle, so that he now only needed to shout, and in this fashion we glided down arguing at the top of our voices. Discussion then had to be abandoned while I climbed up, and resumed when the engine stopped as I changed tanks again, which 'Jacko' at last got over must happen if I kept turning the selector the wrong way!

A year or two later we had a period of mysterious engine failures. The bafflement lasted several months and it was amusing to see the number of experts who came to Old Warden to diagnose the trouble only to retire discomforted. The symptoms were these:– The engine would start as readily as it had always done, and on run-up, rpm and mag drops were normal. Airborne, the engine ran normally for about 20 minutes and then started to miss. If the mags were checked at this stage there was usually no dead cut, but of course the engine ran even more roughly on one mag. It then progressively lost power until height could not be maintained and a forced landing ensued. Then the engineer would come along, start the engine and run it up. All normal. 'Ground tested and found serviceable'!

My first encounter with this phenomenon was en route to a display at Waddington, again with 'Jacko' in the back. It was a gorgeous summer's day, and the engine having died away, we glided down into a convenient stubble field. While 'Jacko' prodded into the works, I lay sucking a straw in the sunshine. The only person to query the goings on was a farm labourer who didn't really understand what it was all about but went away and kindly returned with a flask of tea. We were back in the First War era. The cowlings replaced, 'Jacko' swung the prop and the engine caught and ran up with no sign of a miss or a mag drop.

Setting course once more, it was again about twenty minutes before we missed a beat. In spite of all my juggling with the throttle, mixture and ignition, the power gradually dropped off and I made a one eighty towards Leicester East which we had seen a little while previously.

In fact we only just made it – downwind and with two feet to spare over the hedge as the power died away completely. The story of how we hitch-hiked ignominiously back to Old Warden in the back of a Fairchild Argus must keep for another day.

As it seemed highly unlikely that both ignition systems were failing at the same time, all the early efforts to diagnose the problem were concentrated on the fuel system. Eventually both mags were removed and run on the bench, when it turned out that the insulation *was* breaking down at the same time. As a matter of interest, the R.R. Falcon in the Shuttleworth Bristol Fighter is the oldest Rolls-Royce aero engine still operating anywhere in the world.

As may be surmised from all this, the aircraft has no vices and is a very docile and easy aeroplane to fly. Although it has no wheelbrakes, the braking action of the tailskid combined with a touchdown speed of 40-45 mph gives a very short landing run. In the air, the elevator is light, the rudder very light and the aileron control increasingly heavy with speed. Because of this lack of control harmonisation and the amount of aileron drag, co-ordinated turns without slip or skid need practice if one is used to modern aircraft. It must have needed good co-ordination to sight accurately in a dogfight.

*   *   *

(While this report varies considerably from that of the conventional 'air test', the editor feels that readers will glean some of the atmosphère of flight in one of the earlier true fighting aeroplanes).

*   *   *

*'Jacko': Squadron Leader L. A. Jackson. He was Richard Shuttleworth's first engineer and became Manager of the Collection until he retired in December 1966.

11 The SE5a
Air Commodore A. H. Wheeler

Amongst the group of aeroplanes which pointed the way to the range of fighters in service through the early 1930's, the SE5a takes a very important place. Its in-line (V-8) water-cooled engine of around 200 hp was fully controllable with a normal throttle: the 200 hp available was better than the contemporary rotaries which gave around 130 hp, although they got that horsepower from a very compact engine which was (by comparison) less vulnerable to bullet damage. The Sopwith range of fighters which installed the rotaries were marvellously manoeuvrable; almost too manoeuvrable for some of the less skilled pilots.

However, the 200 hp of the Viper enabled the designers of the SE5a at the Royal Aircraft Factory – later the R.A.E. – to make the structure very rigid indeed and thus to provide really effective aileron controls; by that date elevator and rudder controls were already effective.

That gives the essential picture of the SE5a as a thoroughly manoeuvrable fighter aeroplane with a performance comparable to all other fighters on the Western Front in 1917. It was generally agreed that the controls of the SE5a were better harmonised than most of the other fighters of the time.

To understand its flying characteristics today we must still compare it against the tail-skid/no brakes aeroplanes of the Gipsy Moth/Tiger Moth period since the size and weight were similar.

The SE5a was essentially like a Gipsy Moth with an engine of nearly twice the horsepower. It would therefore swing on take-off if the pilot allowed it to. It was very sensitive to a pilot's mishandling on a landing and would 'bucket' across the aerodrome repeatedly telling him that he was a ham-fisted 'so-and-so': but the engine power available immediately on demand was the clumsy pilot's salvation, so far as his reputation went, if he had not been unlucky enough to do his first bump in front of the Flight Office. To the many pilots who may want to (and to the very few who may have the opportunity to) fly the SE5a, I would give this advice: Above all fly a tail-skid/no brakes aeroplane first. Then treat the SE5a with great respect (amounting to anxiety) when you fly it. Take off and land it on grass. Open up the engine slowly and, very gently, counteract any swing which develops. Don't over-correct; the swing is very gentle.

The lift-off is easy and all manoeuvres thereafter are straightforward. Aerobatics are quite normal and easier than on many 1930-1950 aeroplanes, but true inverted flying should be avoided since the engine carburation and oil system are not designed for it. Barrel rolls and flick rolls can be done easily although the flick roll is discouraged because of the added strain on the rigging. Although the SE5a was designed to dive at very high speeds of around 300 mph, there were records of wings coming off in dives during the First World War, probably due to flutter above that speed. On the Shuttleworth Collection SE5a the maximum speed in a dive should be restricted to 150 mph, which is quite enough for demonstration purposes. This also helps to keep the maximum rpm of the engine within safe limits.

Before the landing, check again and again the slow flying and stalling characteristics of the SE5a. They are not frightening, but they must be respected. The SE5a, like the later generation of Spitfires and Hurricanes, requires a very precise approach speed and very sophisticated handling on the final landing. If you muff the landing, the SE5a will tell you so again and again in front of all your friends for 150 yards, and more if you have to give bursts of engine to try and recover. Perhaps the best recovery from a bad landing is to put the engine on, go round again and then try to persuade watchers that you only intended to do a touch and go.

As indicated above, the Wolseley Viper or Hispano-Suiza engine is a perfectly straightforward V-8 of the design common in many of the high-powered cars on the road today. The Viper was in fact the British un-geared version of the Hispano design

and it gave 200 hp. Engine instruments on the dashboard include an oil pressure gauge, a fuel pressure gauge, a rev. counter and a radiator temperature gauge. All these should be watched frequently, especially the rad. temp. gauge since the radiator shutters are manually operated by the pilot. The fuel pressure gauge must be watched also in case the engine-driven pressure pump fails: in that event, pressure must be restored and maintained by the pilot's hand pump, which can be an arduous job as I discovered when the pressure failed on one leg of the King's Cup Air Race in 1929 and I had to maintain the fuel pressure against a broken pressure pipe for 30 miles to the next check point! The Viper engine is basically very reliable, with its direct drive propeller eliminating the reduction gear troubles and vibration of the geared Hispano.

Take-off and landing speeds, although not very critical, are worth mentioning. Lift-off after about 80 yards in a light wind can be done safely at 50 mph on full power followed by the climb away at 55. A pilot must remember that in the event of engine failure soon after take-off it is not possible – certainly not safe – to attempt more than a 60° turn to find a landing area and the gliding angle must be achieved immediately. This goes for all aeroplanes of that date. Cruising speed can be selected anywhere between 60 and 100 mph with a top speed, quickly attained, of 132 mph. The SE5a was, in fact, one of the first aeroplanes which could be looped soon after take-off and gain height in doing it: this manoeuvre is not permitted on any of the Shuttleworth Collection's aeroplanes! However, no pre-liminary dive is needed to attain a suitable speed for a loop, which can be done neatly from around 120 mph, although first attempts at a loop will probably produce a tidier manoeuvre if entered at a slightly higher speed.

A pilot making his first flight on an SE5a should (as said earlier) spend some time checking the slow flying and stalling characteristics. The stall will occur at about 42 mph and it was normal in the SE5a's operational days to do the approach at about 15 mph above the stall, i.e. a good 60 mph with throttle closed; a drop in speed to about 10 mph above the stall, say 50 mph, could be allowed as one passed over the hedge. With engine on, the approach speed could be lower, but traditionally 'rumbling' in was looked upon as unprofessional: there was the additional value in engine-off approaches in that the conditions obtaining in that condition more nearly resembled those of engine failure, so that a pilot faced with that eventuality found himself in comparable circumstances to his normal approach. Loss of height and speed on the final approach can be achieved by side slip or 'swish tails'. That generation of aeroplanes had no flaps or spoilers, so the normal approach technique then was gliding turns down to 200 ft. then side slip on the straight approach over the airfield boundary, level off at 20 ft. and – perhaps – make a good landing. The landing run on the ground should present no problems (on grass) since the slip-stream from the idling engine is still effective with more if needed and the tail-skid is steerable (with the rudder) as on a Tiger Moth. Landings can also be done with a cross-wind component of at least 7 mph. Like all tail-skid aeroplanes the SE5a should not be landed on a hard runway surface, although the take-off on a runway should present no problems unless there were engine failures on the take-off run.

All in all, the SE5a is one of the most pleasant aeroplanes to fly of all its contemporaries.

12 The L.V.G. CVI

Desmond Penrose

The restoration of this important example of a genuine aircraft of the German Army Air Service of the First World War took over five years of patient research and craftsmanship. Manufactured by Luft Verkehrs Gesellschaft (Air Transport Company) m.b.H. (L.V.G.) at Johannistal bei Berlin it was designed as a two-seat short-range reconnaissance and artillery observation aircraft.

The restoration to flying status took five years and whilst SVAS member Maurice Brett researched the identity, colour scheme and markings, the airframe was rebuilt by Old Warden engineering staff with considerable voluntary help, with Peter Franklin breathing new life into the 230 hp Benz.

By Christmas 1969 the fuselage was nearly complete with new pilot's and observer's floor, a new front bulk-head to support the engine and much of the plywood skin replaced. The wings had been completely stripped of fabric, most ribs rebuilt and all false ribs replaced (over 100 of these) and eight spars capped, top and bottom, with plywood and wrapped with fabric and the framework made square; after a long process of dyeing the fabric to the five-colour lozenge pattern (in two schemes) the wings were recovered. The interplane struts with the aircraft were flat pieces of stick so new ones to the correct shape and dimension were made; the whole of the centre section was completely rebuilt, but using the original spars.

The original fuel tank was corroded, so a new one was made together with a new frame to carry it and, as the original fuel pumps were missing, modifications were made so that Gipsy Queen 3 engine-driven fuel pumps could be used. The engine had been removed and completely overhauled and although little internal wear was evidenced (in fact grinding marks still existed on the cylinder walls) the push rods were bent and new carburettor floats had to be made to replace the missing ones.

The radiator needed a new core and, as the entire radiator shutter system was missing, this was rebuilt from scratch, from a sketch appearing in a 1919 issue of 'Flight'. With the remarriage of the engine and airframe, the first engine runs were made; initial taxy tests and tentative hops started on 29th March 1970, fortuitously a Flying Day at Old Warden.

These early tests revealed a tendency for the coolant to overheat, but this was thought mainly due to the position of the radiator which lies horizontally within the top wing centre section with the air passing upwards through it; it was hoped that greater cooling would be achieved when the aircraft was flying rather than static.

Oil pressure, or the lack of it, was of concern. This was put down, initially, to the fact that 1914-1918 oil was thicker than the more modern detergent oils and so a straight (non-detergent) 120 oil was tried and out went *that* theory as the increase in pressure was slight. It was really a question of re-educating oneself to the fact that oil pressures in Benz's *were* low.

Taxying revealed no major problems; the elevator was responsive, the rudder effective with the tail up, but partially blanked tail down, and the lifting surfaces wanted to get us airborne at 28 mph. No qualitative assessment of the ailerons was possible but all augured well for a safe, if not sparkling, aeroplane. However, much work still needed to be done and with the Shuttleworth Trust dependent on several supply sources for the various components, some of which were made or restored on a voluntary part-time basis, a restoration of this kind becomes (or appears to become) a protracted affair and it was not until 28th September 1972 that the L.V.G. circuited an airfield for the first time in just over 35 years. The first flight, of 4 minutes duration, was piloted by Air Commodore Allen Wheeler and showed that the overheating problem had not been cured. An in-the-field modification which increased the angle and depth of the radiator louvres permitted a second flight of 15 minutes within an hour. The cooling problem still existed and further modifications were carried out to force

more air through the offending radiator. On the next day two further flights, of 45 mins. and 1 hr. 05 mins., allowed completion of the airworthiness requirements and on Sunday 30th September 1972, in a display known as 'Hendon lives again', a crowd of 3,000 at Old Warden saw the culmination of some 5 years' hard work by many friends of the Trust, as L.V.G. CVI 7198/18 diced, very gently, with the Collection's Bristol Fighter.

An enormously spacious cockpit is markedly uncluttered. On the left is the throttle, with a press-button on top for moving through a cruise rpm gate; below the throttle is the advance and retard lever. The broad twin-hand-grip control column has a brake lever at its rear which can lock the elevator in flight. Instrumentation is sparse; A.S.I., altimeter, tachometer, water temperature and oil pressure gauges.

The petrol ON/OFF cock is on the centre cockpit floor and the starter magneto on the right cockpit bulkhead. The louvres to control water temperature are positioned by means of a hand grip situated above the pilot's head on the upper mainplane centre section.

The water temperature and oil pressure gauges are the most scanned; the cooling problem is still with us on a hot summer day and I for one, can't get used to 10 psi. As with the Bristol Fighter an observer, or ballast, must be carried, but only on the initial test flights has ballast been used and only then with loud protests from the engineering staff. Starting is an easy business for the pilot, but requires two hand-linked swingers to turn the 9 ft. 6½ ins. diameter propeller. The Benz is a smooth running engine, even at low rpm, and, with its rhinoceros horn-shaped exhaust which emits black smoke at high revs. (i.e. about 1,400) is not unlike a good steam engine.

Taxying in light winds is straightforward with liberal use of power to keep an airflow over the partially blanked rudder; in winds over 15 mph, wing walkers are required or you are left with the feeling as you weathercock into wind that the rudder was only added to carry the standard size national insignia.

In no wind the take-off run is only 250 feet at a through-the-gate maximum of 1,450 rpm. The ride from the undercarriage is soft with good damping. The rudder is light but not too effective, the elevator light and positive, but the ailerons? Now we know why the control column is two handed.

The best climbing speed is 55 mph which gives an initial rate of just over 850 ft/min. General handling, up to 120 mph, is acceptable but the lack of harmonisation of the controls advertises the fact that this aircraft was meant for straight lines. Only gentle manoeuvres, no aerobatics, to preserve the active life of the aircraft have been flown, but these have advertised a design fault in the shortage of fin and rudder area; this can be aggravated further if the observer is at all bulky or active; a broad shouldered observer swinging the Parrabellum can yaw the aircraft quite successfully. Gentle dog fights with the Bristol Fighter have proved that the front gun is purely for opportunity snap-shots and that defence had to be left to the observer; quite the opposite to the F2b which can be used as a fighter. In 'Flying Fury', James McCudden, who scored a fair number of his 57 victories over L.V.G's, highlights the one occasion when an L.V.G. 'was doing Immelmann turns and half rolling' because it was so unusual. Zoom and dive would appear to be one of the best methods of defence; prolonged dives are not to be recommended as L.V.G.s had a reputation for shedding their wings in long dives.

The maximum level speed is 95 mph (some 11 mph down on 1918 published figures) and the stalling speed 38 mph. No spinning has been carried out; wisely, considering the small rudder and fin. Between these two speeds the L.V.G. is a safe, rather dull and, in bumpy conditions, a physically tiring aircraft to fly. Its major attraction is its uniqueness.

The approach is flown at 55 mph initially, tapering off to 50 mph over the hedge. A fairly positive elevator input is required to achieve a three-pointer and the neck needs craning to see where you might be going; 'might' because once the tail is down and speed decreases below 20 mph, unless there is 10 mph of wind dead ahead you will either weathercock into wind or ground loop, unless you raise the tail and apply a bout of power (not recommended on small fields). Moral: stay friends with the wing-walkers; they may become 'catchers'!

With some inertia and large diameter wheels the ground run, especially if wheeled on, can be lengthy but may be shortened by reducing the normal idle rpm (advanced) of 500 back to 350 by retarding the ignition; only to be recommended when safely down and running straight.

It has been suggested that the L.V.G. flies like a D.H.9a.

Being ex de Havillands I doubt it; all D.H. types were females (and most were ladies). The L.V.G., on the other hand, is all Teutonic; male, purposeful, and not caring much to be diverted from its chosen path.

13 *English Electric Wren*
Wing Commander R. P. Beamont

The Wren was an entry for an Air Ministry competition in 1923 for an ultra-light training aircraft. It was built by English Electric, at Preston, to the design of W. O. Manning, who came back to Warton at the age of 80 in 1960 to see it fly again at the Company's test airfield which was dominated at the time by Canberra jet bombers and the P1 supersonic fighter prototypes.

The Wren was powered by a 398 cc ABC engine which had been developed for a moderate-sized motorcycle, and was entered for the Daily Mail Light Aeroplane competition at Lympne where it achieved a joint class win (together with the ANEC) by flying an astonishing 87.5 miles on one gallon of fuel.

Embodying the relatively new departure for that time of a cantilever monoplane wing, Manning intended that the aeroplane should attain as far as possible the efficiency of a glider; to do this he produced a very clean structure with slim fuselage and a narrow track undercarriage with wheels three-quarters submerged in the fuselage, and with the pilot virtually sealed in the deep cockpit behind the engine by a fabric apron which clipped round his neck!

There was no such refinement as a windscreen, presumably on the basis that the performance would hardly necessitate one, and he was quite right on that score.

In 1955 a small team of wood and fabric workers from the old Vampire production team at English Electric, headed by test pilot Peter Hillwood and development engineer Bill Eaves, had rebuilt the aircraft which is now at the Shuttleworth Collection. This was from components of one aircraft that had been stored in the factory roof at Strand Road, Preston, since it last flew as the competition winner in the 1920s, and from the remains of a second aircraft which had been located on a farm in Dumfriesshire.

The overhauling and rebuilding of vintage aeroplanes requires the three main ingredients: money, skill and dedication, and in the case of the Wren the last two were available in good measure; but the budget was small and when after stripping the engine and replacing valve guides and springs the first engine runs suggested low compression and very little power output, the team had to make the best of it.

Hillwood, a 12-stone 6-footer, provided a formidable load for such a little aeroplane, but after a number of taxy runs along Warton's long main runway he coaxed it into the air for a straight hop.

Reporting that it handled very well in pitch and yaw and adequately in roll, he said that it didn't appear to want to climb out of ground effect and that as expected the landing roll was difficult to keep straight due to the hard tailskid (on the asphalt runway). Taxying could only be done with 'steerers' at the wing tips of course.

Eventually Hillwood got the Wren up to 200-300 ft for circuits on a number of occasions, and so it was decided to try my 13 stone in it!

The pilot sits virtually on the floor of the fuselage in a small and original wicker-work seat, and with the 'apron' round one's neck there is no vision of the stick, throttle and mixture levers and the all-important oil drip-feed valve, so that control is by 'Braille'.

The dominant impression gained is that one's bottom must be almost touching the ground, and that forward vision is restricted by a large ASI and RPM gauge mounted on the fuel tank at the back of the engine, and by the open ends of the two large exhaust stubs at about eye level!

The engine starts readily and runs smoothly but of course noisily at such close proximity, and with a shove from the wing-tip handlers it quickly gathers sufficient speed for adequate rudder control. Then the narrow wheel track makes itself felt by early rolling tendency which is easily controlled with aileron, and the tail must be raised to take-off attitude with positive forward stick as there is clearly insufficient power for prop wash to raise it unaided – and here is the first problem. With such marginal power the effect of increased drag is large and immediate; too coarse use of elevator, rudder and ailerons can so reduce acceleration as to prolong or even prevent take-off.

On my first flight at a maximum take-off RPM of about 2,150 and in almost calm air speed built up with the tail high to about 27 mph and appeared to stick there until about $\frac{1}{2}$ mile of runway had passed, then at about 28 mph I felt the wheels stop rumbling. Holding it level, speed built up very slowly to about 34 mph and then as I eased into a gentle climb, dropped rapidly to 27 again. We then stopped climbing and were in the classic situation of running out of runway but with insufficient height to turn. So very gingerly we traded the height gained from 100 ft back to 50 ft regaining speed to 34 mph and then eased up to attempt a stabilised climb at 30 mph. This in fact worked and a just-positive climb was maintained at 29-30 mph until back at about 150 ft, and now outside the airfield boundary.

Warton is on low marshland but has buildings and hedges, etc., surrounding it, and I had never before realised what mighty obstructions to aviation these were!

It was apparent that the RPM was fading at this point and that a normal circuit was not going to be achieved, so keeping control movements to the bare minimum I eased into a turn to starboard – and immediately started losing height as the induced drag increased.

Deciding that a circuit was not going to be possible and that it was a case of first things first I kept the turn going and descending until after 180° we were heading back at the boundary with a positively enormous tree just ahead (in fact a 20 ft tamarisk bush). Diving off the remaining height directly at the bush temporarily restored ASI to about 32 and permitted a hop over the bush at the last moment into the clear flat plain of the airfield, and even though downwind in a very light breeze I hoped that we could at least regain the runway.

At this point and now very low over the grass we started to fly again and I realised we were benefiting from ground effect, but max RPM had now dropped to 2,000 due to overheating and it was simple to organise the aeroplane with its surprisingly responsive controls and excellent stability to a gentle landing which only ground-looped slightly at the end due to the 5 knot

tail wind.

In subsequent flights with the oil-drip feed properly controlled to prevent overheating we managed to maintain up to 2,300 engine RPM and established that with its clean aerodynamics, long tail arm and generous control surfaces the Wren had basic longitudinal and directional static stability and neutral lateral stability, and that these together with good pitch and yaw response and good harmony in stick forces added up to a very pleasant and conventional aeroplane, that is in all but the power/weight ratio sense. But the diminutive Delphine Grey Fiske whose skill and attractive 8 stones or thereabouts enabled her to get the Wren up to practical circuit height at will, was the only pilot who managed to demonstrate the Wren effectively at public displays in the 50s, providing at the same time a pleasant distraction for the professionals of the Warton test centre.

In 1975 the engine was worked over at Old Warden by Wally Berry who succeeded in restoring it to 2,500 RPM at which, in the capable hands of Desmond Penrose, it showed take-off and circuit capability from the Old Warden grass together with a maximum level speed of 40 mph, stall buffet at 24 mph and no untoward characteristics in a shallow dive to 70 mph. All quite remarkable for a 55-year-old design and on only 3 nominal hp.

The Wren has shown itself to be a very pleasant, straightforward aeroplane in the air, but primarily that with an engine of twice the power it could have been a very likeable little sporting aeroplane.

It was a remarkable design achievement and much ahead of its time.

14 The de Havilland D.H.51
David Ogilvy

Before the Moth series became established as the most historically significant mass-produced light aircraft of all time, much heart-searching must have been carried out at the de Havilland stable at Stag Lane. The Moth did not just happen to happen, for immediately before it were two designs each at the opposite ends of the light aeroplane range. Between them, these machines showed clearly that neither quite filled the bill to serve the needs of the prospective private owner and amateur pilot.

Despite its design number, the D.H.51 surfaced later than the D.H.53. The 53 first saw daylight under its wheels in late 1923 and made some impact at the Daily Mail light aeroplane trials at Lympne in October that year. It covered 59.3 miles on a gallon of petrol, but with an all-up weight of only 565 lbs. it was too small, too low-powered and proved generally inadequate for serious touring. The 750 cc Douglas motor-cycle engine with which it was fitted gave constant trouble.

By contrast the D.H.51 was relatively large, with a span of 37 feet and a permitted weight of 2,240 lbs. Everything about it was big, with a sensibly roomy cockpit and accommodation for three in tandem, although it became more established later in a two-seat configuration with a detachable fuselage panel over the front 'hole'. Although powered at first by a 90 hp R.A.F. 1a engine, this did not suit the airworthiness authorities of the time and greater success came when power was standardised on the V-8 Airdisco.

This engine is quite interesting. Basically a war-surplus Renault, it was acquired, modified and marketed by the Aircraft Disposal Company, which, of course, provided the basis for the type name. Producing 120 hp in its civilian form and ideally suited in power output for a machine of the 51's size and weight, it was of greater overall calibre than needed for the popular-to-be light aeroplanes of the twenties. As a result, the Airdisco was virtually sliced down the middle and each half produced the basis for the A.D.C. Cirrus 1, which with its four upright cylinders in line produced 60 hp in return for a weight of only 290 lbs. This came to power the first D.H.60 Moth in 1925, but that is a separate story.

The first D.H.51 to fly, in July 1924, was G-EBIM. It spent much of its life in Australia and after conversion to a floatplane capsized in Sydney Harbour at the age of seven. The second, G-EBIQ (the letter Q is no longer used in registrations) survived only a little longer to be scrapped at Hanworth in 1933. The third and last (in all senses) had – and indeed has – a much greater claim to a place in the history book.

G-EBIR first flew in September 1925 and early in the following year went to Nairobi to become the first aircraft to be registered in Kenya. Registration systems changed with the expansion of civil aviation and after four months in which 'IR flew as G-KAA, Kenya was allocated its own prefix and this long-lived machine became VP-KAA for the next 43 years. Through a cooperative venture which included considerable help from Hawker Siddeley Aviation (as successors to the de Havilland Aircraft Co.) 'KAA was airfreighted home to England for permanent preservation by the Shuttleworth Collection. H-SA refurbished G-EBIR at their Hawarden (Chester) works and, after a long time away from home, the last D.H.51 came back to live only about 40 miles from where it had been built 50 years previously.

As a two-bay biplane with a relatively shallow fuselage, the D.H.51 has a strong external resemblance to the famous D.H.9 of World War I, which proved so successful in a variety of post-war civil roles. A large four-bladed wooden propeller gives the 51 a certain added character which helps to augment the impression of size.

With a V-8 engine the 51 has long pipes running down both sides of the fuselage. There is a hinged flap on the left side of the front cockpit to make passenger entry more straightforward than that for the pilot, who has no such facility. The bucket seats have fixed upholstery and these provide a level of comfort that I have not met in any other open-cockpit type, while the spade-grip control column (surely not original?) gives an almost fighterish impression. Vintage-style instruments, few in number, but with large traditional dials, cover the basic needs of airspeed, height, engine power and oil pressure. Other trade tools within easy reach are a cheese-cutter for fore-and-aft trim, acting via a spring balance directly on the elevator, and a pair of pull-for-on fuel cocks for main and reserve supplies which just come from different levels in the one tank, of 30 gallons capacity.

Start procedure is unusual for a light aeroplane that was intended for private use. Although the propeller can be hand-swung, the rapidity with which the four blades follow each other creates an added hazard. The Airdisco boasts a third (starter) magneto; current for this is generated by energetic winding from within, whilst engineers perform a rather similar external cranking operation in slightly slower motion. Although an established method for getting some of the heavier engines into action in the twenties and thirties, it is one that is more normally associated with military aircraft.

Once running, the Airdisco is a smooth operator when within its 'happy' range. G-EBIR has insisted on retaining a flat spot near the low end of the rev. scale, for although adjustments to carburettor balancing have moved the trouble area both up and down the scale, it refuses to be eliminated. But many engines have settings that are best avoided and this one makes no bones about the bits that it dislikes.

On a cold start oil pressure rises to a bare 30 lbs. To a modern mind this is cause for concern, but once the engine gets warm the situation seems serious. However, there is no need for alarm, as the Airdisco (like its successor the Cirrus) has a splash as opposed to pressure-fed oil circulation system and a data plate provides consolation by quoting 5-8 lbs. as the normal operating range. This, however, is at the front of the engine and cannot be seen by the pilot. The engine heats quickly and prefers to avoid long ground running. When long runs are essential for test purposes, a special ground-use cowl can be fitted to deflect an increased air supply to wherever it is needed.

Most tail-skid, brakeless aeroplanes can create taxying problems, but the D.H.51 generates its own. Normally a skid is fixed to the sternport (as on the D.H.60 Moth) or it is movable

with the rudder (Tiger Moth) and the latter arrangement makes the taxying task much easier; G-EBIR though, has a floating, bungee-balanced skid which points in the direction that one has been, but offers little hope or help for where one wishes to go. In practice, though, this behaves more effectively than it feels.

Once the problem of alignment has been overcome, take-off is easy. There is very little swing tendency and the 51 unsticks on its own when it is ready, which is quite soon. Climb performance is creditable with a return of nearly 800 f/p/m. It is during the early flight stage that a recent modification, or more correctly a re-conversion to original, shows to great advantage. When G-EBIR arrived at Old Warden it had the most immovable and purposeless set of ailerons imaginable. One pilot described the feeling as though they were set in concrete, while I feared on my first flight that I had taken-off with control locks in position. This, I thought, must have been a prime reason for the type failing to sell.

How wrong I proved to be. During a routine inspection, a Shuttleworth engineer discovered that all the fittings existed for setting-up differential ailerons, although at that time they were set to travel in equal amounts both ways. What a transformation. With no handbook or other guideline, the sensible solution seemed to be to use Tiger Moth figures. These worked admirably; through no fault of the designer, what had been a dull and uninspiring machine to fly became a living thing. If flown in proper biplane tradition with sensible rations of rudder, the newly-activated ailerons provided a control balance that made turn entry and exit into remarkably smooth sequences.

There is nothing very special about the D.H.51, except that it is unbelievably docile. Unlike the little D.H.53 which indulged in some sharp practices including aileron snatch just before the stall, the larger machine seems to have no aerodynamic vices. The stall, which provides one of the best indications of any aeroplane's manners, is almost indefinable as a precise occurrence. From a leisurely entry the 51's nose eventually finds its way down at a figure below the minimum reading on the ASI, (where there is a +10 position error). Clearly a modern altimeter would show signs of unwinding, but only by using a bit of determined effort and 'entering with intent' can a positive and pronounced breakaway be induced. Even then the wings remain on the level.

Performance is unexceptional, but adequate. With 1,800 rpm the cruise is about 90 mph, but to achieve this the eight cylinders drink about 11 gallons per hour. Range and endurance, though, are adequate with a maximum flight time of about $2\frac{1}{2}$ hours.

With an approach at 55-60 mph IAS the landing holds no surprises, but the large wheels and low pressure tyres offer a far more comfortable touch-down and subsequent roll than the first D.H.60 Moths that followed so soon after. Certainly the 51 will not tolerate a crosswind and the natural weathercock tendency is accentuated by the strange tail-skid attachment that I have mentioned already.

As my original assessment of the reason for the D.H.51's market failure was so grossly wrong, I must assume that sheer size maimed its chances. By the volume of materials alone it must have cost a lot to build; hangarage bills would be high; the large engine drank fairly heavily. All these misfortunes add up to tell a tale that is easy to understand, but as G-EBIR really is such a likeable flying machine, it is unfortunate that customers failed to materialise. The D.H.51, though, was definitely not a failure. It proved the need for a smaller, less expensive and lower-powered aeroplane and from this was born the D.H.60 Moth. Nothing could have been more successful than that.

15 *De Havilland D.H.53*
Humming Bird

Desmond Penrose

Built to compete in the Daily Mail Trials at Lympne in October 1923, the D.H.53 was the first true light aeroplane produced by the de Havilland Aircraft Company. A low wing, single seat monoplane, with a wing loading of only 4½ lbs. per sq. ft., it was powered by a Douglas 750 cc motor-cycle engine as this was the maximum capacity permitted by the competition. Two identical prototypes were built, 'Humming Bird' and 'Sylvia II' (later G-EBHX and G-EBHZ respectively). Both competed at the trials and though neither won a prize, and the engines were unreliable, the D.H.53 was the only entrant to gain a production order; the loops and rolls of Hubert Broad (in Humming Bird) had brilliantly demonstrated the stoutness of the aircraft.

The production aircraft were powered (or should one say under-powered?) by the 26 hp Tomtit inverted V, 2 cylinder engine manufactured by Burney and Blackburne Engines Ltd. This gave a maximum speed of 73 mph and a range of 150 statute miles. This was publicly demonstrated when Alan Cobham flew on 8th December 1923 from Stag Lane to the Brussels Aero Exhibition in 4 hours; much publicity was made of the low fuel cost of 7s 6p (37½p). But was it a truly practical flying machine? Even the press-on enthusiasm of Alan Cobham was dampened on the return flight when, due to a headwind, he was overtaken by a Belgian goods train! He landed at Ghent and had the aircraft dismantled and returned to Stag Lane by boat from Ostend.

The R.A.F. needed a cheap communications and single-seat trainer aircraft and the low operating costs of the 'Humming Bird', as the type became named, seemed the answer in an environment of defence cuts (plus ça change!). Eight aircraft were ordered and deliveries started in June 1924, with the 7th and 8th Service 53's (J7325-6) being specially modified for carrying out launching and recovery experiments from the Airship R-33 (G-FAAG). Again the lack of practicability of an underpowered (military load 71b) light aircraft is evidenced by the R.A.F. striking all eight D.H.53's off charge in 1927. Six came on the civil register to join the remaining (first) prototype, but their impact was slight. To cure the twin vices of lack of power and unreliability both 32 hp Bristol Cherub 3 and 35 hp A.B.C. Scorpion engines were substituted for the Tomtits and, in Australia, a 40 hp Aeronca was fitted as late as 1937. The Shuttleworth Collection's D.H.53 is powered by an A.B.C. Scorpion engine and has been an irregular (though occasionally spectacular) performer at Old Warden Flying Days since it was rebuilt by the de Havilland Technical School in the late 1950's, after being discovered by Squadron Leader L. A. Jackson in the back garden of a house in Eastrey, Kent.

Only fifteen D.H.53's were built, of which three went to Australia, one to Czechoslovakia and one to Russia. If a large production run is an indication of an aircraft's value then the 53 was not rated high, but like the D.H.51 it did have a necessary part in the evolution of that most important and endearing of light aircraft ... the D.H.60 Moth.

One doesn't get in to the cockpit of the 53, for it's more like pulling on an old seaboot; once in, it is not uncomfortable, but just rather cramped, with the cockpit sides in constant touch with the shoulders. Instrumentation is sparse with a highly polished brass single magneto switch dominating the instrument panel. The Humming Bird has never had a good reputation for easy starting (more a bad reputation for frequent stopping) but if the exhaust pipes, like a ram's horns on either side of the nose, are sufficiently well doped with fuel and the swing on the metal propeller vigorous enough then the pilot is rewarded with a cacophony of pops and bangs, accompanied by occasional yellow flames from the exhausts and cries from the ground crew to 'keep it going'.

The overall impression is one of noise and vibration; not noise that implies power – just noise. There is no great leap forward against the chocks as the throttle is opened for this aircraft; just more noise of a more even note. The vibration is

such that vision of the instruments is blurred; maybe it will be less noticeable in the air? Is this how the vibrating winged brightly coloured Humming Bird got her name? Taxying on anything other than well mown grass requires lots of engine (notice I don't say power) with occasional tail raising; not to see where one is hoping to go, for the nose does not obscure the forward view as there is practically no nose, but solely to try and reduce the undercarriage and tail-skid drag. The wheels are of a ridiculously small diameter and the smallest hummock can prove a major obstacle. One is reminded of Captain A. V. C. Douglas who preferred to take his D.H.53 (purchased in 1929 for £50!) off down hill but found 'the poor little machine could not climb the hill with me in it. I used therefore to set the throttle and, tail-skid in hand, proceed to my point of departure, à la motor mower, pushing where necessary!' In its favour, though, the D.H.53 has a good, all round view and a soft, well damped, undercarriage with an effective rudder in low ground speed/high rpm conditions.

Take-off is a very easy though rather protracted exercise. The secret is to get the tail up as soon as possible to reduce aerodynamic drag; there is no tendency to swing but due to the lack of nose reference the exact attitude initially is difficult to judge. This, a well-known test pilot amply demonstrated when, clad in bone-dome and full flying kit, with his broad, 6 ft. 1in. frame overlapping the cockpit, he unsuccessfully tried to get the 53 into the air; all he managed was an impression of a noisy, slightly erratic, two-stroke mouse. I tell the story as he told it to me; subsequently killed test flying, wherever the t.p's Valhalla is I'm certain Peter still tells that story against himself.

Leaving the ground at approximately 40 mph (accuracy is not possible as the vibration makes the A.S.I. needle a blurr) with the left throttle hand determined to get more revs than the Scorpion can give until a safe height is reached, one is pleasantly surprised to find that the Humming Bird is not a bad flying machine after all. Noisy and sadly underpowered yes, but with crisp, powerful ailerons and a responsive elevator and rudder. In fact harmonization of the controls is good, and one can understand how Hubert Broad looped and rolled these many years ago, to the delight of the crowd. However it must have been mainly downhill! 'HX is not aerobatted now, in keeping with the policy of the Shuttleworth Trust, but in the past it showed itself a most agile performer (provided the engine kept going) with loops, barrel rolls and steep, very small, diameter turns at low level.

Maximum speed in level flight is around 65 mph at 2,400 rpm; a comfortable cruise rpm of 2,200 gives about 57 mph. No wonder Geoffrey de Havilland after flying one of the 53's from Stag Lane to Lympne realised that, though delightful to fly, even with the engine 'all out' they were under-powered.

A throttle-back stall occurs at about 42 mph; warning of the approaching stall is by slight aileron tramping starting at about 45 mph and this can lead to a very positive aileron snatch. A comfortable speed on the approach (engine on or off) is 55 mph; the glide angle is rather flat, but the view is excellent and the 53 can be accurately positioned. Three-point landings are easy with the positive elevator and low ground angle of the undercarriage, and the ground roll, after touchdown, is very short due to the combined high drag of the small main wheels and tail-skid.

What overall impression is left with the pilot as he taxies at nearly half throttle, up the sloping NW/SE runway at Old Warden? Relief that the engine kept going on this none-too-popular aeroplane? An aeroplane which even at de Havillands in 1924 aroused 'the very strongest feelings of no-enthusiasm'. Possibly, but if so I would hope he would also realise that the merit of the 53 lies not in its own qualities, but in the refinement of the design process that resulted, ultimately, in the D.H.60 Moth; without the Humming Bird there would have been no Moth. For myself the 53 is as previous de Havilland men found, 'non-habit forming'. The only time the engine failed on me it was courteous enough to do so over a disused airfield, but it has been less friendly to others. Designed to a wrong specification, it is nevertheless an important historical aeroplane and probably the oldest prototype still flying in the world; and what course would British light aviation have steered if there had been no Moth to follow?

16 The D.H.60X Moth
David Ogilvy

When in doubt, compromise may provide the only satisfactory solution; the de Havilland D.H.51 had proved to be too heavy and cumbersome to make any form of market impact, and the D.H.53 which (despite the numbering) went before it had suffered from an opposite set of shortcomings. Therefore something in between was likely to make the grade. The result was the D.H.60, or the first of the Moths, the prototype of which flew from Stag Lane in 1925.

If ever a compromise was a total success, perhaps the Moth was the greatest. Certainly it saw daylight at the right time, for light aeroplane clubs and Government subsidies to go with them came to life in the same year. Until then, most private flying had been carried out in surplus World War I military types, which though strong and pleasant to handle, were alarmingly thirsty for the personal pocket.

Originally fitted with the Airdisco (ADC) Cirrus 1 of only 60 hp, the first Moths were light enough to perform quite well despite such low power, but progressively larger engines were used and the basic Moth layout developed in a number of ways. The original hard undercarriage with a straight-through axle and large, thin wheels with low pressure tyres gave way to a more tolerant split unit with wheels of smaller diameter.

This is where the Collection's Moth comes in. Built in 1928, with a Cirrus engine, G-EBWD came to Old Warden in 1931 as Richard Shuttleworth's first aeroplane, which he used as his personal fly-about. Shortly after acquiring it, from Brooklands, he remotored it with a Hermes of 105 hp, a move which all members of the present team of pilots fully endorse! Although the first Moths had their exhausts on the left, on

'WD the long pipe runs alongside the right-hand side of the cockpits and entry from the left is normal practice. Getting aboard, although straightforward when compared with the problem on pre WW1 types, is not the easiest of exercises, especially for the front seat, for which it is necessary to climb over, or almost through, a flying wire; taking the usual care to tread only on the strengthened walkway, on arrival there is no hinged flap to increase the small size of the 'hole'. However, all Moths built from about 1930 onwards incorporated this helpful entry/exit facility from birth.

The cockpit itself is small, both in width and length. It is very much more cramped than that of the later Tiger Moth. There is insufficient room to put a worthwhile cushion behind one's back and still have the stick and instruments sufficiently far ahead for comfort. However, this is a petty penalty to pay for a machine with so many virtues.

An uncluttered panel, or dashboard as it would have been called, contains essentials only; an airspeed indicator graduated from 40 to 160 mph, an rpm gauge, a cross-level and a pre-ICAN non-sensitive altimeter complete the picture. An early P-type compass graces the floor, while a generous rear hatch holds sufficient to make 'away matches' practicable. The person in the front is allowed to read height and speed only, but has the added benefit of a large clock with which to criticise the pilot for failing to make his ETAs!

Starting the Moth is simple and traditional in style: a normal hand-swing by one person, with the outside fuel tap on and the throttle set as the only essential checks. However, before, during the sucking-in operation and after starting, the uncowled upright engine provides visual entertainment, as the rockers and valves are exposed for all to see and generate an almost hypnotic effect to watch from the cockpit.

Unlike the earliest splash-fed Cirrus engine which offered about 5 lbs. of oil pressure, the Hermes operates at a more comforting figure and jumps to about 60 lbs. after starting, settling to an average of 38-42 in normal flight. It produces a unique sound, with a series of rapid hollow 'pops' from the end of the long pipe.

Taxying calles for mild patience and a touch of the fast-dying traditional skill. Again unlike the Tiger with its steerable skid connected to the rudder, the pure Moth has a fixed stem

attached rigidly to the bottom of the sternpost. This offers little help in negotiating corners, for which generous rudder accompanied by careful bursts of engine may need to be supported by the use of appropriate aileron. I hope that I have succeeded in explaining the procedure for this in chapter 2.

Brakeless aeroplanes have the associated problem of needing to have the engine well throttled back in order to avoid excessive speeds on the ground. This means that when stationary, carrying out the brief but nevertheless essential checks or just waiting for take-off, the engine cannot be opened-up to prevent the plugs from fouling. Fortunately the upright layout of the Hermes helps to prevent the Moth from suffering too much in this respect, but this is one of the few occasions on which pilots wish for fairly long grass, the tufts of which act as natural chocks.

The take-off is most satisfying, for the Moth's weight/power ratio is good and after an immediate tail-rise it is airborne as rapidly as any of the other conventional light biplanes in the Collection. It is impossible to record a precise unstick figure, as the ASI comes to registered life at 40, but I am convinced that G-EBWD takes little persuasion to fly happily at about 5 mph below this.

Some aeroplanes ride through bumpy conditions with little concern, while others actively disliked rough weather. The Moth falls into the second category, so soon after take-off (if not before) it is possible to assess whether the flight ahead is to be enjoyable or just tolerable. In fact the Moth is unusually sensitive to bumps, so conditions can make it into two almost entirely different aeroplanes. When all is calm, there are few (if any) machines nicer than a Moth, and it can be flown with encouraging precision, but in the rough it can be quite unpleasant.

One of the first tests for any type is to check its conduct at the stall. If it shows unhappy qualities at the low end of the speed scale this serves as a warning, calling for added caution, but the Moth emerges with an entirely clean health record. In fact there is little to report except to state the expected; the ailerons become as sloppy as one would anticipate, there is a lot of waffling and wallowing and eventually the nose drops (at a speed below the lowest ASI graduation) in an unhurried manner. With the usual variations and a few built-in tricks a wing can be persuaded to go down, often to the tuneful accompaniment of a whistling in one or more of the wires. At this stage any minor irregularities in the rigging make themselves seen, heard or felt – sometimes all three. But the machine behaves impeccably.

What is the Moth really like? Although very capable of serving a fully functional purpose and with some very long, famous historical flights to the type's credit, it is in another sphere that it shines today. To enjoy the purest pleasures of flight just for the sake of flying, the Moth is hard to beat. The ingredients must be available and the time must be right, but let us choose a calm, clear June evening, about an hour before dusk, and with nowhere particular to go. With the Hermes throttled back to provide a gentle 1,500 rpm (the data plate quotes 1,900 as normal) and the ASI offering a little less than 70 to match, I will leave the rest to the imagination of the reader, except to add one personal point; to gain the full rewards of such a situation this needs to be a solo affair and an empty front cockpit adds a certain flavour to the scene. That may sound ungraciously unsociable, but there is something special about flying alone and many pilots will understand what I mean.

In general handling the straight-winged D.H.60 Moth is quite different from its successor the Tiger. The earlier machine has a more taut feel, especially to the ailerons, which are a little heavier (offering more resistance to roll) than those of the D.H.82a, but are totally lacking in the latter's slight slop. Certainly the Tiger is more manageable in rough weather, when its additional weight must help.

The D.H.60 loops very neatly, and can be flown all the way round positively from about 110 mph IAS, but is not ideally suited to any manoeuvres in roll. Straight wings with blunt tips, only one (lower) set of ailerons with restricted travel and other traditional biplane features all add to this limitation, but it does not detract from the pleasure. A normal pilot wants to roll only when the aeroplane that he is flying virtually 'asks' to be rolled. The Moth does not do that.

Clearly a biplane with all the usual array of struts, flying and landing wires and other excrescences that make it what it is, will not gain much performance on the level with power increase, but a bigger engine offers positive benefits in the rate of climb. Although I am writing primarily about the Collection's

Hermes-engined G-EBWD, a direct speed comparison between the first and the last of the D.H.60 series brings home the point; the original 60 hp Moth claimed a book maximum of 91 mph while the later Moth Major, with its 130 hp, offered 112 – or roughly a 20 percent improvement from a 100+ per cent power increase. This means, of course, that 'WD is hardly any faster now than it was when built with a Cirrus, but its get-up-and-go climb performance (it clocks more than 650 feet-a-minute) vastly improves its overall qualities as a flying machine.

Moths lived at the peak of the era of side-slipping, which provides the most effective way of killing surplus height on the approach. The Moth slips well, which is a useful facet as its normal glide is far from steep. Crossing the boundary fence at about 55 mph IAS sets-up 'WD nicely for a steady hold-off. With the earlier large wheels, low-pressure tyres and axle undercarriage the Moth bounced energetically after only a minor misjudgement, but the system now fitted is more tolerant. Nevertheless, if one must err – and who doesn't? – it is advisable to round-out a little early; the subsequent drop onto three points is far less embarrassing than the bounce that is given free of charge in exchange for a slightly premature touchdown during the hold-off. The rudder remains reasonably effective almost to the end of the landing run, but although the fixed skid helps to provide braking and straightening, out-of-wind landings should be avoided if possible.

Aeroplanes leave impressions that may not be directly related to their true qualities. Types with controls that are well balanced in both feel and response almost invariably appeal to pilots, but often other features override some of the more obvious points. The Moth's ailerons are heavier than they might be and out of all realistic proportion to the lightness and rapid action of the elevators, yet this obvious disparity seems lost among all the more favourable features. Thousands of pilots have flown Tiger Moths and many dozens still do so; I have met a few who dislike the Tiger, but I have not heard of any pilot who has failed to enjoy flying the true Moth. That is what the Moth is all about.

17 *The Hawker Tomtit*

John Lewis

The Hawker Tomtit was designed for a competition held by the Air Ministry to select a training machine for use by the Royal Air Force. Although of entirely conventional design and appearance the aircraft was unusual in that it was of all-metal construction. This feature, allied to very careful attention to detail and fittings, enabled a very low all-up weight to be achieved, so that a brisk and useful performance could be obtained from a modest power output. The pupil's cockpit was equipped with a hood, which could be pulled forward, and which completely precluded an outside view for the occupant. This arrangement was made so that the then new science of flying on instruments could be taught. The power unit is an Armstrong-Siddeley Mongoose radial of 150 bhp.

The Collection's Tomtit was, in fact, the last one built, and civil registered G-AFTA. It was given to the Trust in 1959 and has appeared regularly in displays since then. Before that it was operated by the parent company, and was often flown by the world-famous Chief Test Pilot of the time, Squadron Leader Neville Duke. It is the last remaining airworthy example of the type in the world.

Although of all-metal basic structure, the whole airframe, with the exception of the cowlings is fabric covered. Perhaps the most unusual feature of the design is the large positive stagger, which was incorporated partly for aerodynamic reasons, and partly so that the occupant of the front seat might the more easily bale out should the need arise. Both cockpits are capable of being fully equipped, but for centre of gravity reasons, the solo pilot must occupy the rear. The view is good from either, except that in the tail down attitude the nose and motor succeed in hiding a fair bit of the view directly ahead. The cockpits are roomy, the seats reasonably comfortable; and all the major controls fall readily to hand.

There are negative G. hoops on the rudder pedals and the operating range of the various controls is small enough to make them easy to operate in any manoeuvre. The instrument fit is modest but sufficient, with all the basics supplied in the cockpit, and a sight glass fuel gauge in clear view forward. The windshields are small, but they work well. An unusual feature, although quite normal for the time, is a hand operated starting magneto, with a separate switch to operate it, on the right side of the instrument panel. A Kigass primer for enrichment prior to starting is also fitted. The undercarriage is conventional, with sprung mainwheels and a steerable sprung tail-skid, but the mainwheels are a long way aft and give the impression that the aircraft will be very light on the tail in ground handling. This is in fact the case, and it is one of the Tomtit's least forgiving traits.

The Mongoose is a five cylinder radial, fitted with twin ignition; and is normally aspirated through a carburettor. It is a left hand tractor, and is fitted with a two-bladed wooden propeller. This motor has a large displacement of nearly nine litres, but has low rotation speed (max 1,780) and has a modest output of 150 bhp. It is accordingly quite efficient and uses only about 7 gallons of fuel per hour. It is otherwise unremarkable, except that many of its parts are interchangeable with those of the Lynx and Jaguar powerplants of the same manufacturer, a pleasing piece of standardisation from an earlier age.

There is something peculiarly appealing about a radial. As motors, they are impressive in their own right and they seem to dominate the aircraft fitted with them. During the walkround pre-flight inspection the pilot finds that even the Mongoose, small though it is, impresses in just this way. It is impossible not to be satisfied simply with the look of the thing. The checks on it are standard enough, however, and consist of the usual search for signs of damage, gas and oil leakage, blown plugs, cowling and exhaust input security. There are a lot of cowlings in the Tomtit and it is easy to miss one should it have become insecure. The consequences of this could be severe, and this check is done with great care by both engineer and pilot. The remainder of the walkround is mainly concerned with fabric condition and the tension of flying and landing wires, and is common to all aircraft of this class.

Climbing into either cockpit is quite easy, using the footsteps provided, but as is the case with all biplanes great care is needed. A careless step, or a slip, and the luckless individual lands on the lower wing, doing considerable damage in the process, and perhaps going straight through. Once in, however, the straps are fished out from below the seat, where they always fall in among the control runs, fastened, and a run through the cockpit checks is done. The controls are exercised first, with the exception of the rudder (which is held pretty firmly by the skid when the aircraft is at rest), the fuel turned on and the throttle checked for full and free movement. There is no electrical system to worry about, but both magneto switches and starter mag switch are double checked off before the fuel system is primed and the propeller handled.

Starting a big piston is a art. Starting does not appear to respond either to good design or to science – but to climate and to engineering knowhow exclusively. Unless I know a motor really well, not only the type but also that individual specimen, I prefer to take advice on this topic. The amount of priming is crucial, and if the engineer says 'six strokes', six strokes it gets, no more and no less. Accordingly, with the requested amount of prime carried out, the throttle is set – just a fraction open on the Mongoose – and the two prop swingers link hands and walk the prop to a position just on the compression, ready to start. When they are safely out of the line of the prop, the lead man, who is actually usually the one holding the blade, calls contact, and all three mag switches are put on. The pilot then chants a steady countdown – three two one NOW, and the two swingers pull the blades over as fast as they can, at the same time running well clear. Fractionally after the NOW, and this is vital; also fractionally after the prop has begun to turn, the pilot cranks the starter magneto by hand as vigorously as he can. Too soon with this and the prop could swing back and injure the hand of the starter, too late and the opportunity to fire may be lost. In fact, if everything is well, the motor will fire, kick over and gradually run up as the cylinders all begin to catch. Sometimes the prop will kick back and fire the motor in reverse when the starter mag is operated. This is not always a failure, however, as frequently the rotation will result in

another firing which will kick the prop back the correct way and running will be established, provided the starter mag is kept in operation. Once the motor is properly caught in all cylinders, and a reasonable fast idle established, the starter mag is switched off and for the moment the pilot can relax. There are always snags, of course, and in this case the snag is the hand-cranked starter magneto. It is awkwardly placed and stiff to turn, and to ensure a good spark intensity must be turned rapidly. It is essential to wear a glove, or skinned knuckles will inevitably result. The reader who uses tools will know already the exquisite pain of a skinned knuckle. It is enough to say that carelessness here can spoil enjoyment of the subsequent flight.

The typical radial single big end is very hard worked, and oil pressure must start to build very shortly after the start if damage is to be avoided. Accordingly, the very first start check is to see that oil pressure has risen. This is slow at first, as the relief valve is opened by the cold sluggish oil, but must at least start to indicate within 30 seconds and should be at its normal working range of 75-90 psi within one minute. Provided this has occurred, the fast idle of about 800 rpm is now increased to about 1,000, to hasten the warm-up and improve cylinder wall oiling, while helping to offset the danger of oiled plugs. Radials tend to be oily motors in any case, as the lower cylinders are always subject to draindown. This causes the clouds of smoke attendant on every start, and care is always necessary to avoid plug fouling at low power, even when the motor is warm.

Despite the apparently ideal configuration, radials are never smooth. This is largely due to the single big end assembly with its large out-of-balance rotating mass. They tend therefore to have a low frequency galloping vibration oddly reminiscent of a big single motor-cycle, and it is nearly always a surprise to the newcomer just how rough they are. The Mongoose is no exception to this rule, and as the warm-up proceeds the pilot is aware both of the vibration which shakes and blurs the airframe and of the peculiar exhaust beat of the 5 cylinders. Even at this modest power, moving the elevators in the nosedown sense causes the tail to become alarmingly light, although the pilot is in the rear cockpit, and it is evident that someone will be necessary to hold the tail down for the run-up. When the oil temperature has risen to 15°C, therefore, one or two men hold the tail down, the chocks are checked and the motor run-up to full power. This normally gives about 1,650 rpm. Power is then reduced to an intermediate setting, and the mags checked individually to see that there is a drop as each is switched off (this is important; if there is none it may mean that the mag has failed and was never on in the first place), and that the drop is about equal and of a reasonable size. If all is well, the idle is checked at about 600 rpm, the chocks waved away, and the aircraft is ready to taxy.

Taxying the Tomtit is easy. The steerable tail-skid enables very small radius turns to be made with rudder and a little power alone, and without using tricks such as aileron deflection, and stopping first. The response of the motor to throttle is immediate and gentle, and only a trickle of power is needed even in long grass. The weaving necessary to ensure that the area ahead is clear makes for an untidy appearance, but is absolutely essential. The long exhaust pipes keep fumes away from both cockpits, and the pilot can look out beyond his windshield without the risk of being soused in oil. It is, however, absolutely vital to remember to hold the stick hard back, especially if any amount of power is to be applied. Checks at the marshalling point are quite simple and consist of the usual items plus a check that the tail trim is neutral. The slats are permanently locked in and can be ignored.

The Tomtit is a very light aircraft, and acceleration once full power has been applied is brisk. The tail lifts off at once, unless it is deliberately held down, and the swing resulting from the application of power is small and very easily countered. A special feature is the comfortable ride given by the long travel under-carriage, and this plus the long nose make holding the chosen take-off attitude simple. In fact, the aeroplane leaves the ground very quickly, before even the airspeed indicator has reached the start of its scale, and climbs rapidly out of the ground effect. At once the handling feels good, and the pilot feels quickly at home even if he has not flown the aircraft for some time. The best rate of climb seems to occur at about 65 mph, and at this speed also the control power is adequate to cope with gust-induced disturbances, although the roll-rate obtainable from the single ailerons is modest.

In the cruise the aeroplane settles nicely on to about 85 mph, and at maximum power well over 100 mph is available. Even at these speeds however, roll-rate is still modest, and full aileron applications generate very large amounts of adverse yaw. Further, turbulence also gives rise to large yawing motions, and the accompanying sideslip sends the slip bubble shooting wildly from side to side. Since the aircraft side area is large, this gives high side forces on the pilot as well and makes the ride uncomfortable. It is clear that the Tomtit is a little loose directionally, and would have benefited from rather more fin area. Fortunately, the rolling moment generated by the sideslip is not too high, so this characteristic is not very much of an embarrassment. It does make the aircraft a little unhandy in a display, however, if turbulence is more than slight. This, and the large wing area and low roll power also require that only small angles of bank be used over the trees or near the ground, lest a bank upset occur which may need more space to correct than is available. For these reasons the display handling of the aircraft in turbulent conditions will seem to be rather restrained.

In contrast, the elevator control is delightful. The response to elevator inputs is crisp and precise, with the aircraft adequately damped, and the force gradient nicely harmonised with that of the ailerons. In fact, the pitch handling of the aircraft is its nicest point, and it is evident that this will make for tidy landing characteristics. The stall is docile, with the aircraft remaining stable and controllable right down to speeds below those which can be shown on the ASI. When the stall does occur, either wing may drop, usually in response to a side-slip allowed to develop in the last few seconds of the deceleration, but control remains in all axes and recovery is immediate on lowering the nose. The motor keeps going reliably throughout all manoeuvres provided positive G is kept on, and the whole aeroplane feels taut and reassuringly strong.

Landing the Tomtit is not only relatively easy, but very pleasant as well. It shares with comparatively few other aircraft, one of which is the Tutor, the characteristic that its handling in the landing phase is so pleasant that the pilot enjoys the process to the full, rather than viewing the whole matter with a fair degree of arousal. All good landings start with good approaches, of course, and the approach handling of the Tomtit is exemplary. Speed stability at 65 mph, with a small amount of power set, is excellent and in calm conditions pilot workload is very low. Turbulence produces problems of course, as already described, but the increased lateral damping available in ground effect minimises these, and the first class pitch handling enables very exact touchdowns to be made, cushioned by the good undercarriage. Directional control during the roll-out is the only problem, as stability reduces once the tail is down and power is reduced to idle, but the steerable skid helps, and the aircraft slows rapidly, as the low tickover speed of the Mongoose gives little residual thrust. The landing distance required is short for an aircraft not equipped with brakes, and this enables it to be landed directly into wind irrespective of runway. This is preferred because, although perhaps due to the aft setting of the wheels the aircraft can cope with small crosswind components, it is definitely easier and safer into wind; and a really good swing, once begun, is unlikely to be corrected on a brakeless taildown aircraft.

The Tomtit is a genuinely pleasant aircraft, with thoroughly good handling qualities and virtually no vices. In fact, delightful though it is, one may feel perhaps that it is just too good for a training aircraft, where to teach well the instructor needs a craft with a nice balance of vices just obvious enough to be of value without being downright dangerous. It is a fact, of course, that it shares this characteristic with its successful competitor, the Tutor, and also with the much later Chipmunk and jet Provost. To my mind, though, a trainer should have a few more teeth than this genuinely nice machine possesses. It was just this balanced set of vices which made the Harvard and piston Provost such excellent trainers, and so enabled the pupils trained on them to accept more readily the awkwardness of the higher performance aircraft to come. Nonetheless, as a machine to be enjoyed, and as a beautiful little aeroplane, the Tomtit remains a delight, and is loved by all who are fortunate enough to fly it.

18 The Avro Tutor

David Ogilvy

Serious and organised pilot training stemmed jointly from the Smith-Barry system and the Avro 504 series, which as a basic type had an uninterrupted career from 1913 until outphased in the early thirties by the Tutor, born of the same parents. Not surprisingly, therefore, the Tutor first saw daylight with a background that gave it a healthy position in the field of competitive contracts. By the time it became hardware in regular Service use it had little if any excuse for revealing serious shortcomings, but even in the later seventies it has much to boast, for it can claim several relatively up-to-date features that were missing from the type that succeeded it. When considering a production light aeroplane of the period, who thinks in terms of efficient brakes, a tailwheel that usually faces the right way, roomy cockpits with adjustable seats and rudder pedals and an all-flying variable incidence tailplane?

In vital statistics the Tutor cannot be measured as anything but a tough horse. With a span of 34 feet, an all-up weight of 2,400 lbs. (tare 1,722), a fuel capacity of 32 gallons and a 7-cylinder Armstrong-Siddeley Lynx radial engine developing 215 hp (which along weighs more than 500 lbs.) anyone can be forgiven for conjuring thoughts of an operational aeroplane, rather than a trainer that saw extensive use with Flying Training Schools and University Air Squadrons of the period. Economically, regarding both initial purchase and operating expenditure, this massive beast must have proved unpopular with those whose lot it was to protect the Service purse, but for the more fortunate being whose task was to instruct or be instructed in the type, the Tutor could have produced few complaints.

All that is in the past, so let us look at the Tutor today. The lone surviving specimen, K3215, served with the RAF College at Cranwell from 1933 to 1936, when it was transferred to the Central Flying School; unusually it remained on Service strength and was used for various duties until the end of 1946, but eventually became civilianised for a short career as G-AHSA. During the film 'Reach for the Sky' it suffered a crankshaft failure and for several years difficulties over engine replacement kept it grounded. However, a nationwide purge produced three specimens of the Lynx in various states of disrepair and, from these, one good unit was built-up by Armstrong Siddeley of Coventry.

From without, the Tutor can offer several features of practical merit. Basically an all-metal aeroplane with a fuselage structure of welded steel tube with fabric covering on wooden stringers, the one-piece side panels, each running along the entire length of the two tandem cockpits, can be removed for ease of inspection and servicing. The engine, too, is easily accessible and much routine maintenance can be carried out without removing the Townend ring that surrounds it.

Once aboard, the aeroplane's relatively massive bulk again comes to the fore, for I know of no other light aeroplane with individual cockpits that can offer such an encouraging amount of space and comfort. Yes, comfort! The rudder pedals are easily adjustable for distance and the bucket seat travels up and down through a range to suit the whims and reach of any pilot of any size. An enormous trim wheel and a thick brake lever, which can be set-up on the notched basis, add to the atmosphere of size and solidity that accompanies everything about this machine.

Starting offers the first and only inconvenience, for in keeping with the traditions of the time and in common with most other Armstrong-Siddeley radials, the Lynx is brought to life via a starter magneto (which necessitates a third ignition switch) and some energetic hand-cranking from within. If, as has happened many times, a pilot straps himself in tightly before this stage, he may have difficulty in reaching the cranking handle which is on the right wall in front of, and reached from under, the instrument panel. In fact the Tutor offers a choice of three alternative starting methods, including a dog on the front of the propeller to engage the cross-head

from a mobile Hucks starter, but today's standard method is far more basic. Two men, with hands linked, prepare for a hand-swing and, after all the normal setting-up has been completed, the pilot calles 'one, two, three, go'. On this last word the swingers swing; the pilot turns the crank as energetically as its inaccessible position allows and he keeps turning until the engine fires steadily. Then he switches off the third magneto. As an alternative to hand-swinging, an engineer can activate things by winding an external cranking handle. There are, of course, a few other things to do such as remembering to switch-off the priming cock, which cannot be reached at all from the rear cockpit without standing upright! An intriguing feature of the Lynx and its sister engines, including the earlier Mongoose in the Tomtit, is that they will run happily whilst turning either way; it is not uncommon for an unsuspecting pilot, who at first sound thinks all is well, to see the engineers' hands waving for him to switch off and try again in the hope that it will obey its left-hand tractor specification at the next attempt. Presumably the Tutor could be taxyed backwards when in this mood, but commonsense and the desire for long engine life must prevent pilots from indulging in anything more than minimum running time in this condition.

At this point we revert to relative normality. Oil pressure rises to about 90 lbs./sq.in. and on a radial it is particularly important that it should do so fairly quickly, then we wait for some positive action by the oil temperature gauge before the run-up, for this engine likes a heavy oil (straight 100 is used) which keeps the consumption to an acceptable figure. With a thinner grade, such as 80, the oil usage escalates by about 100%. As most radials, the Lynx runs slowly and a full-power check gives only 1,675 rpm or so, while the makers' recommended cruise figure is a remarkably precise 1,620 rpm. Once on the move, the efficient brakes, which are as good as those of a Chipmunk and far better than those of the Magister, which is one of the types that replaced the Tutor, provide a pleasant surprise to anyone who has flown other (mostly brakeless) machines of the period.

The weight reveals itself on take-off. Despite an alleged 215 hp, acceleration is remarkable for being so unspectacular; the entire ground run is fairly ponderous, but only a little guidance is required for keeping straight and once the Tutor is airborne it seems to be relieved of its troubles and settles into a tolerable climb rate of 750 feet per minute against a book figure of 1,000. It bangs its way commendably through the bumps and behaves best if left alone, for at slow speeds the ailerons are not as responsive as they are light; this is despite a generous ration of both surface area and number, for they are fitted on upper and lower wings.

The cruise is comfort itself. The cockpit space provides scope for an airborne picnic, if required, but equally it offers really worthwhile space for the more conventional pastimes such as furling and unfurling maps. It is sensible to keep goggles on as a secondary windscreen, but the one fitted to the aeroplane is sufficiently workmanlike to permit periodical doses of bare-eyed flight. A typical radial cruise setting of 1,600 rpm gives 90 mph on the dial.

At lower speeds the handling characteristics are not outstanding and certainly not crisp. Understandably this is most marked at the 65-70 mph IAS on the climb, but an airspeed increase of only about 20% produces an aileron response, in terms of movement required in relation to rate of roll, that is much more alert. Throughout the speed range, though, control displacement is unusually marked and in snappy reverse-direction turns the control column really moves across most of the width of the broad cockpit. However, there is more overall control improvement with speed increase than the unwary pilot might expect from the initial sluggishness, for from a little more than normal cruise of 90 mph the machine can be rolled into and out of turns with some spirit. This must have been a marvellous asset for any ab-initio instructor whose task was to teach the varying effects of controls and subsequent exercises at different airspeeds.

Aerobatics are kept to an absolute minimum; in the interests of long life of both airframe and engine (which must always be to the fore in a pilot's mind throughout any flight) a restriction of one loop per demonstration flight and no manoeuvres that involve negative G has been imposed on this and the majority of Shuttleworth machines. As a result, one does not indulge in prolonged series of aerobatics either for practice or personal pleasure; no doubt those who flew Tutors regularly when there were plenty more reached quite high standards (and certainly the C.F.S. team members who specialised in inverted formation achieved this) but from the odd loop or two I can claim neither expert knowledge nor a clear conscience to investigate. The machine is extremely pleasant to fly and, of all the earlier types held at Old Warden, it is by far the most practicable and satisfactory specimen for general and cross-country work; it is the oldest machine of all that can tolerate a fair cross-wind for landing and can be taxyed anywhere without help, but it does not ask specifically to be aerobatted, especially when compared with today's counterparts the Bulldog and Chipmunk, which do. As it is a heavyish aeroplane, airspeed diminishes rapidly in the first part of a loop and it is easy to run short of it at the top; if one makes this mistake – and, alas, I know from experience – nothing drastic happens, but there is a strange and protracted feeling of empty nothingness as the machine seems to flop its way round into the descent, but still very considerately facing the right way.

A feature that finds the underlying truth in any aeroplane is its manner at and near the stall. Here the Tutor is very kind; perhaps too much so for a trainer. As airspeed decreases, a marked control woolliness displays itself, especially with the ailerons, but despite this they are usable down to the breakaway, which occurs at 42 mph IAS. From a gradual, level approach to the stall the result is very tame, with a fairly positive nosedrop but almost no tendency for a wing to go down. If put to the test in slightly less textbook conditions, such as a more rapid movement in pitch and a spot of built-in yaw, slight spirit displays itself and I have no doubt that if left alone, it would enter a spin; respect for the Tutor's age, though, has meant not waiting to find out.

The big trim-wheel is heavily geared and a lot of winding is needed to produce a small change in tailplane incidence. This means, of course, that large movements are called for in order to remove stick loads, which are more than moderately pronounced with changes in airspeed. Not surprisingly, this is most noticeable between level flight and a glide approach and shows most at the end of a demonstration flight, when the average operating speed has been a little higher than that of a routine cruise. Changes in power, too, create moderate load changes.

Generally the view is good in all directions, but the exhaust collector ring and its external cowling protrude well outside the fuselage line and this creates some visual obstruction on the final approach and hold-off. However, the landing itself is completely uncomplicated, for a gorgeously soft undercarriage absorbs most of the loads that one may place upon it. Although the Tutor *can* bounce from a premature touch-down during the round-out, its general tolerance is most comforting. In normal conditions there is little tendency to swing during the landing run, although the tailwheel encourages a longer roll than might be anticipated; if needed, though, brakes provide solutions to both situations. General reactions are very favourable. Everyone who has flown the Tutor likes it. It is a gentleman's aeroplane in its roominess and docility, while the powerful response from the ailerons at the high end of the speed scale helps to produce a positive feeling of being in control of the situation. Assessing it as an aeroplane to fly, it qualifies as excellent; judging it as a trainer on which to teach, it fails to object sufficiently strongly to minor mishandling, so an instructor might not find his pupils' (not students in the thirties!) errors standing out as glaringly as they should. As a significant historic aircraft – and the world's sole survivor of the type – it holds a high place.

19 *The Granger Archaeopteryx*
John Lewis

The Archaeopteryx was designed by the brothers Granger, two lace manufacturers, who had in mind learning to fly; and who wished to design and to build an inherently stable aeroplane and to do this as cheaply as possible. The design itself was inspired by the tail-less designs of Dunne, which at the time were making a big impression on the aviation world. The structure was checked by a professional stress engineer before build, and was pronounced safe to 4 G. The aircraft flew successfully for some four years before being laid up and stored, and achieved its aim of allowing the brothers to learn to fly. It was later presented to the Collection by Mr. R. J. T. Granger, when it was rebuilt and test flown in 1971. Since then a modification programme has been carried out, and the aircraft began appearing regularly at Shuttleworth displays in 1975. In the meantime Mr. Granger and his son saw the aircraft fly on test, at a special invitation ceremony, and pronounced themselves delighted to see their gift to the Collection once more in the air.

The aircraft is a swept-wing tailless design having a fuselage and a single conventional fin and rudder. The wing is parasol mounted and has the reflex trailing edge cambered section normally considered necessary for a tail-less design. Two large struts brace the wing at about half-span each side. The undercarriage is bungee sprung and is mounted on vee struts below the fuselage, with a conventional tailskid at the rear. Longitudinal and lateral control is achieved by elevons which are in fact moving wing tips, pivoted at about their quarter-chord point, operated by a system of push rods through a mixing control from the control column. These move symmetrically as elevators and differentially as ailerons. The column moves fore and aft for longitudinal control and has a wheel segment mounted on top which is rotated for lateral control, whilst the rudder is operated by conventional pedals. The cockpit is extremely small, and access demands that a section of the top fuselage decking is removed, then replaced once the pilot is in. So small is it, in fact, that the throttle has had to be mounted externally so that clearance exists for the control wheel, and the pilot lies rather than sits in the machine, feeling as though he is wearing it. The motor is a Bristol Cherub of 35 bhp, driving a two-bladed wooden airscrew, and fuel is gravity-fed to it from a tank in the wing centre section.

The tank, which holds about 5 gallons of fuel, is filled, the oil level checked and the pilot starts his walk round inspection. Of particular interest is the security of all the detachable panels, the condition of the airframe in general, and the full and free movement of the elevons and rudder. During this inspection one is reminded again of the small size of the aircraft and of its tiny motor and propeller, and of the minute dimensions of the cockpit. With the cockpit aft decking removed the simple canvas hammock seat can be seen, in which the pilot lies rather than sits, and the few instruments available, airspeed and rpm indicator on the panel, with the altimeter flat on the floor between the pilot's legs. It looks as though the altimeter at least is going to be difficult to see. After carefully easing oneself into the cockpit, and with the top decking replaced so that the shoulders are supported, the error of this assumption becomes at once apparent. It is not difficult at all; it is impossible. Furthermore, with the throttle outside on the left, and the snug fit of the control wheel under the coaming, it soon becomes apparent that flight handling is going to have to be an elbows outside exercise. The view is splendid in every direction except upwards and forwards, in which direction the wing hides absolutely everything. It is clear that the view into a turn is not going to be all that it might be, but straight down and behind it is superb.

Liberal priming, through a special pipe to the cylinder heads, is necessary when the motor is cold, together with a few turns of the propeller to suck in the rich mixture. A long stretch from the cockpit to a tap high on the centre section struts turns the gravity-fed fuel on, and, with the throttle set about $\frac{1}{3}$ open, the single ignition switch on, and with a bit of luck, the motor fires

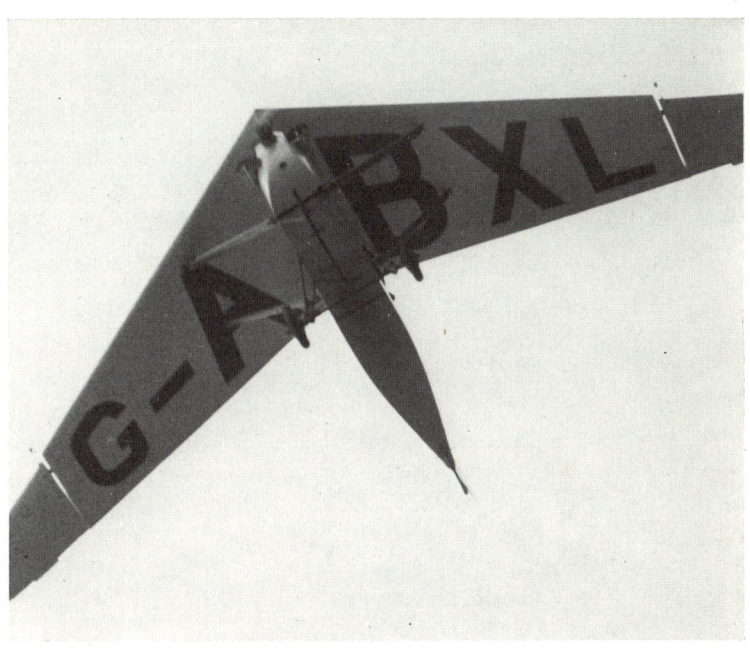

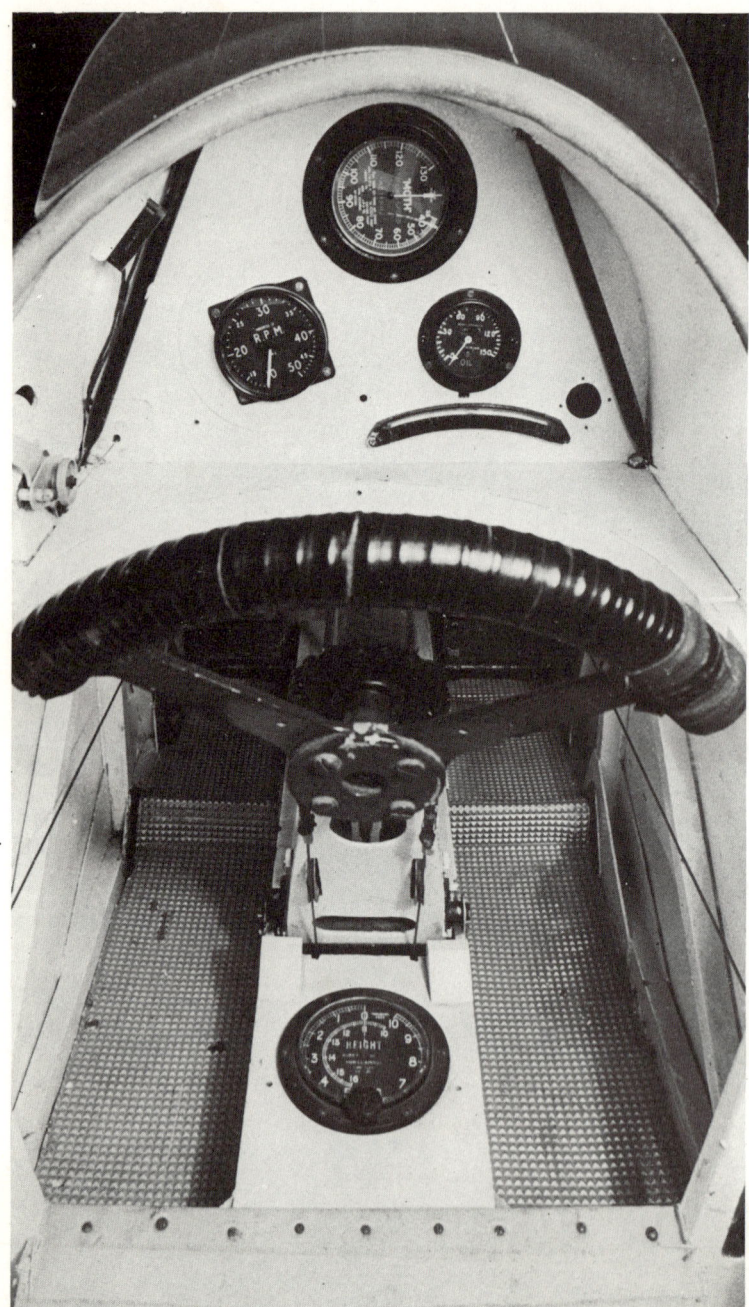

first pull of the prop and settles down to a steady 1,200 rpm tickover. The noise from the stub exhausts is a steady bark, and vibration, due perhaps to the very light wooden prop, is fairly marked. The windshield does not do a lot of trade in these conditions, and usually the pilot feels the need to use his goggles, although sliding lower into the cockpit does help a bit. After some four minutes running it is assumed that the heads are thoroughly warm, and that the oil is beginning to thin, so a full power check can be done. With a single ignition system the only purpose of this is to make sure that a reasonable rpm is available, and so if 2,800 or thereabouts shows, the pilot is content, and the motor is throttled to check the idle. Provided this is satisfactory at about 800 rpm, and that the motor picks up cleanly from low to high power – this is needed during landing, of which more later – all is well and the time has come to taxy.

The aircraft has no brakes, but slows down readily when power is removed due to the tailskid drag. The tailskid is fixed, but the wide-chord rudder gives excellent low-speed turning capability when power is used, so ground manoeuvring is never a problem, even in 10 knot winds. About 1,600 rpm is needed to hold a fast walking pace, and this turns out to be the ideal taxying speed, as under these conditions quite vigorous turning is possible with recourse to further power increase.

The aircraft is unhandy in a cross-wind due to the narrow undercarriage track and fairly strong natural lateral and directional stability, and so we always take off directly into wind. Being low-powered, and having a fairly high wing loading, it also requires a lengthy take-off run, so that the actual position for the start of the take-off run has to be chosen with some care, bearing in mind that the climbout gradient is pretty modest too.

Once lined up, full power is applied immediately and the aircraft quickly gathers way. Because the elevons are out of the slipstream, the aircraft cannot be put into the 'tail up' attitude until flying speed has very nearly been reached. Further, since the aircraft is so short-coupled, virtually no longitudinal damping is available, so that any pitching oscillations generated by the mainwheels will be virtually unopposed. From both these considerations it will be seen that the aircraft is best left in the 3 point attitude and allowed to behave as it will during the roll. The undercarriage has bungee springing but no damping, so energy absorbed is returned largely undiminished. Indeed, bumps in the grass cause the most hair-raising kangarooing motion, over which the pilot has virtually no control. Until flying speed has been reached each bump acting on the wheels, which are rather far forward, causes a violent pitch-up and the aircraft is thrown into the air, with the nose initially pitching up rapidly, which is followed by a ballistic flight path with the nose dropping until the wheels once again touch and the whole process is repeated with increased amplitude, until mercifully, flying speed is gained, and the aircraft can be maintained in the air and speed further increased such that the climb may begin. The trouble is that if an aft stick input is made in an attempt to remain airborne before speed is sufficient, and the aircraft touches again, the combined nose up pitching moment of elevators and under-carriage reaction leads to a pitch rotation rate of at least $5°$/second, which in the nose up sense just at take-off is absolutely terrifying, and would certainly lead to the loss of the aircraft if it were unchecked. The rotation can be checked by crisp action with the extremely large elevators, but it takes extremely fine judgement not to overdo it and to touch again with even more horrifying results, and so the preferred course of action is to sit tight with the elevons in about the cruise position and await being fired off the ground in earnest at a high enough speed to guarantee success. This solution was learned after early tests showed that the extra drag of the deflected elevons only prolonged the take-off roll, and in addition worsened the handling problems already discussed. Wind is the major factor in alleviating this problem, as a good 10 knot head component reduces the ground speed accord-ingly, and reduces also the energy going into the undercarriage during the roll. During early tests, though, a number of other fixes were tried, with varying degrees of success, and it may be of interest to describe these.

When the problem was first identified during the pre-flight test hops after the rebuild, our first reaction was to suspect the centre of gravity, and this was moved a small distance, and the hops repeated. A small improvement resulted, but not nearly enough to be a cure. Lengthening the undercarriage – the original had larger wheels – to increase the ground incidence, and moving the wheels aft, was a considerable help, as was softening the tyres by reducing pressure to about 12 psi. The most powerful fix, however, was to increase the elevator up travel until stick clearance against the pilot was only about 1 in. The combined effect of all these changes has been to render the aircraft manageable in non-turbulent weather conditions, but it still requires considerable skill, and more than one pilot has been badly shaken by its handling characteristics, which are quite outside the range of that found on more conventional aircraft.

Once in the air, the handling is more relaxed, but still unconventional, with some features which occasion considerable surprise. For example, with the pilot's elbows outside the cockpit, the rate of climb at 70 mph indicated is very nearly zero once ground effect is cleared. On the first flight, the low speed handling being unexplored, I was attempting to climb at 70 mph, and was still below 200 feet some miles from the airfield, and small turns reduced this. If I was not to have to fly all round the world in order to land back at Old Warden, it was clear, something would have to be done. After a while, inspiration struck and I retracted my elbows into the cockpit. At once, a gentle climb began, and all was well, but it still took 10 minutes to reach about 600 feet. A propeller of slightly larger diameter improved the excess thrust situation, however, and although performance could never be said to be sparkling, both take-off and climb have benefited from this modification.

In fact, the shape of the drag curve is such that climb speed is not critical to a few mph, and anywhere from 58 through to about 70 mph a fairly reasonable rate can be had, provided the pilot keeps his head low and his elbows in. Speed is measured by both a standard ASI and by a wind-operated pressure plate mounted outboard beneath the starboard wing. Either gives reasonable results, but of course neither has been calibrated for pressure error, so what the actual speed is under any given conditions no-one knows. This is not important, however, as you can imagine, provided there is consistency and reliability, and this has been the case.

The minimum speed which has been achieved is about 51 mph IAS in a gentle dynamic pitch-up, and about 54 mph under stabilised conditions. This is quite a high speed for a landing on rough grass, as it represents a lot of energy to get rid

of in an aircraft as unhandy on the ground as the Archaeopteryx, but the senior low speed aerodynamicist at RAE
Bedford said that on no account should we stall it, and this is as
far as we intend to go. The true stall in tail-less aircraft – as
opposed to the minimum stabilised speed often mistaken for it
– can be highly dangerous as total loss of control and tumbling
can result, without a chance of recovery. At 51 mph the stick
force is strongly nose up – due to the pitching moments on the
elevons – but the aircraft itself is still stable, and sufficient nose
down control power exists to generate a brisk nose down rate
on selection. It is in fact a characteristic of the configuration
and aerofoil section that the basic wing pitching moment
remains largely constant throughout the incidence range, but
this is not so on the biconvex section of the wingtip elevons,
hence in part the stick forces. At the other end of the speed
range we have achieved 105 mph IAS in a shallow dive, and
whilst the basic aircraft has again remained stable, the elevator
hinge moments have reversed, and the pilot has to oppose a
strong nose down elevator load. In this condition also,
however, the basic aircraft is longitudinally stable, and a
healthy nose up pitch rate can be generated by an aft stick
input. Although the wingtip controllers are generously mass-
balanced, since there is no information on flutter, and on such a
configuration a flutter problem would be extremely serious,
this is as far as we intend to go in this direction.

No pilot-operated elevon trimmer is fitted, so it is not
possible to influence in flight the elevon hinge moments fed to
the stick, but two fixed bias tabs are fitted to the trailing edges,
so that by trial and error a position can be found between
flights which removes the load and puts the aircraft in trim at
any chosen speed. We have found that the natural cruising
speed of the aircraft is about 85 mph, and that this is also a
good speed for displays. We have, accordingly, arranged for it
to be in trim at that speed. Because of its extremely low
longitudinal damping, and thick high lift wing, however, the
aircraft has a wicked gust response, and in turbulence this can
make the pilot feel most insecure. As the gust is struck, the
increment or decrement of G takes place as normal, but it is
larger than expected for the wing loading and speed of the
aircraft, and the nose shoots up or down 5 or even 10 degrees,
seemingly in an instant. Turbulence is therefore not popular,

and on rough days the aircraft is not flown.

Laterally the aircraft is also unconventional, in that it has largely neutral stability; that is to say it will remain at almost any angle of bank in which it is left for some time, at least until spiral instability makes itself felt. Unusually, also, the elevons are also without any special trail characteristic in the turn, and once the deflection used to initiate the bank has been removed, there the aircraft stays with no force required to hold it either into or out of the turn. This characteristic gives it a curiously dead feel, which is at once belied by the powerful response if the controls are moved. Sideslip, if applied using the rudder, results in very strong sidewinds in the cockpit, a very large speed error induced in the pitot static system; and very little else. In fact a small roll rate is generated, but by much the largest effect is the change in longitudinal trim caused by the cross airflow.

All the controls are very light in the air, and extremely powerful. Because of the large elevon area, vigorous use of the controls results in a rapid speed loss, and large nose-up inputs are accompanied by tremendous drag increases which quite overpower the small motor. For this reason all manoeuvring has to be restrained, but the low speed of the aircraft gives small turn radii in any case, so this is not too obvious in displays. Much of the time in a display the motor has to be kept fairly close to full power, and this produces a deafening racket in the cockpit, even through a padded flying helmet, as the stub exhausts give no silencing whatever. They also emit two black trails of smoke pretty well throughout the power range. This is because the little motor is worked very hard and we prefer to run it a shade on the rich side so that cooling is guaranteed, rather than try to get it spot on and perhaps have the motor tighten up.

The landing is undoubtedly the most precarious part of the whole flight. Induced drag at low speed is very high, and the final approach is flown with about $\frac{1}{3}$ power at about 60 mph. As a last gesture to deception, the Archaeopteryx now settles down to a beautifully steady final approach – it just seems to like that configuration. All this just goes to lull the pilot into a false sense of security, and renders him thoroughly ill-prepared for that most critical phase of any flight, the landing.

The roundout is commenced at a wheel height of about 10

feet, and it is easy, using those enormously powerful elevons, to fly the aircraft level just above the ground. The throttle is closed, and – this is the critical bit – the aircraft held off the ground just an inch or two until it will fly no more. This usually occurs in ground effect at about 50 mph. Touch inadvertently before this and the aeroplane rockets up into the air, pitching nose-up, just as in the take-off. Touch a bump at this speed, or drop it in from 1 foot or more, and it does it anyway. As speed further reduces, no pilot intervention is successful and it must just be ridden out, the impacts increasing in violence until with diminishing speed and energy the oscillations gradually die out. Of course, if things start to go badly wrong early enough in the roll-out, the best solution is to apply power and to go round again. Later on, however, this is not possible as the violence of the impacts lifts the fuel in the carburettor and causes a rich cut. On about one in two of such landings the motor cuts dead and stops; on the others it has to be run at idle for some minutes before the over-richness clears and it can be run up to give enough power to taxy. When asked, none of us can ever bring himself to blame it.

You may feel that the Archaeopteryx emerges from this article at first sight as a supremely awkward aeroplane to fly, and one in which all the bad habits imaginable are combined. In one sense this is so, and yet, this is only partly the truth. Operate the aeroplane only in calm conditions, into wind from a dead smooth runway, and most of its really unpleasant habits are countered. In any case, one must realise, most of these habits belong to tail-less aircraft as a group and not to this one uniquely. The astonishing thing about this remarkable little design is that it was produced by two people who were without formal design and aerodynamic training, and who then proceeded to test it and learn to fly in it using only common sense and engineering know-how. Put this way the achievement is seen for what it is, an astonishing story of success; and the aircraft a triumph of the first order. We are all proud of it, and we hope that you will be also when you see it flying.

20 The Miles Magister
David Ogilvy

When Britain had an almost all-biplane Air Force, the Miles Magister caused a number of eyebrows to rise; an elementary trainer that was a low-wing monoplane, with power-operated flaps, brakes and a tailwheel, opened an entirely new era in the world of military aeroplanes. Destined to operate alongside the Tiger Moth at Elementary Flying Training Schools before and throughout World War II, the M.14 Magister had been developed from the earlier Miles Hawks in much the same way as the Tiger had evolved from the original Moths.

Altogether about 1,300 Magisters were built in England (plus another 100 or so in Turkey) and the type could be seen making circuits appear like hornets nests. In the early war years, without R/T, aerodromes could handle traffic in quantities that everyone considers impossible with our relatively empty skies of today; in 1941 the EFTS at Burnaston, Derby, had 108 Magisters on strength and of these more than 70 were put in the air almost every day, with the use of just one satellite landing field to relieve some of the congestion. First solos, too, were slotted into all this, with instructors usually choosing the relative quiet of the lunch hour when the numbers in the circuit were down to a dozen or so.

It was in this environment that the Maggie, as the type was affectionately called, really came to be known. But scenes change quickly, and in 1968 when the Shuttleworth Collection at Old Warden started a serious search to find one the choice was very thin. Altogether eight were traced, with six in England and two on the Continent, but all were structurally sick and efforts were made to find the one with the greatest prospect of early activation. The Collection was about to acquire one from

Norfolk when, quite by surprise, a private owner at Shoreham had set about putting a specimen into flying condition and, as he was due to be posted abroad and could not take it with him, he offered his machine for sale. The Collection found a kind sponsor who paid for it and so came G-AJDR; but it was not 'JDR, for various searches through documents and the number on the fuselage data plate revealed it was a machine unentitled to any civil registration. So 'JDR was struck off the register and the machine reverted to its original pre-war Service serial P6382. Although flown into Old Warden, on arrival the Maggie hopelessly failed a Shuttleworth technical inspection and a year's efforts in the workshops followed before it saw daylight under its wheels again.

The Magister is a mixture. Some pilots were not particularly fond of it and certainly it failed to find the love that the purists poured on to the Tiger Moth; it had a few vices and one or two marginal design features, but for all these sins those who got to know it well found it a most acceptable partner. At the time there was nothing to touch it for ability to carry on in rough wind conditions (it could continue a full training programme when all Tigers were safely locked in their cages) or for a sensible cross-country speed of 110-115 mph. For circuits and landings, with flaps that worked, trim changes that needed counteracting, a tendency for an occasional swing or to lift a wing half-way along a crosswind landing run, it could hardly be bettered. On upper-air exercises it dropped a wing at the stall, spun readily if given the mildest opportunity and stayed in the spin until recovery was effected positively and precisely. In short, a trainer of trainers. I had the good fortune to instruct on the type for a while and I regretted its retirement.

Let us revert, however, to today. With two minor detail exceptions P6382 is in every way equipped to 1939 standards, complete with Gosport speaking tubes, which are difficult to use effectively but cannot fail suddenly. There was an ignition master switch that enabled the front-seated instructor to isolate those in the rear cockpit, with obvious benefits for his peace of mind, but this is missing from 6382; also, a later but wise modification has made it impossible to select both fuel tanks ($10\frac{1}{2}$ gal. in each wing) at once, for when the contents on one side were low it was possible to obtain air and sudden silence in rapid succession. Fuel is lifted from the tanks by two

engine-driven pumps, one of which is used manually for pre-starting flooding.

Starting is as standard for a hand-swung Gipsy Major. When the engine is running the only unusual check is that on the pneumatic flaps. A small knob on the lower left side of the cockpit moves horizontally fore and aft, with a groove in the middle for selecting neutral; a small arrow runs in a similar direction to indicate the setting of the flaps, but they move rapidly and any intermediate position is hard to catch correctly. Taxying is easy when the brakes are evenly matched, but they need adjusting, and usually taking up, far more frequently than would be acceptable in service today.

The take-off is usually a flaps-up affair, but if conditions call for some assistance, partial flap is more easily selected when the system has been exercised a few times each way; then the vacuum tank becomes tired and things move sufficiently slowly for a reasonably accurate setting to be caught. This is advisable when the available run is short, for in nil-wind conditions a Maggie with full tanks and two occupants tends to hug the grass far longer than you would expect.

Once clear, however, the acceleration is healthy and 70 mph IAS produces a climb of about 700 ft/min, with a need for a fair ration of left rudder to fight slipstream. In this condition the nose is fairly high and the ailerons are not really responsive, so when height is not urgent the modern tendency for a virtual cruise-climb at about 80 mph is less demanding.

In the cruise the Magister really becomes two aeroplanes, for as speed increases the differences in comfort and view between front and rear positions become more marked. The front is encouragingly draught-free and sustained flight without goggles is quite practicable, but the turbulence that the front screen and hole provides for the person behind causes him to need a larger windscreen, which still fails to provide any measure of still air. Also, plastic screens tend to become scratched and into a low sun they are opaque in the extreme, so the occupant of the back seat (the pupil's position) has a much harder time than does the person who would be teaching him. Perhaps this is as it should be, for often the instructor was required to spend most of the day aloft while each student had time to warm up and dry his eyes between flights. Unlike the Tiger and many other tandem machines, the c.g. range on the

Maggie permits it to be flown solo from either cockpit and I recommend the front; except on aerobatics (when it was hard to keep up the nose if the rear seat was empty), a slight shortage of backward trim on the descent with full flap is the only penalty. Except in this full-flap condition, when it is longitudinally unstable, the Magister is stable about all three axes.

Using a gentle 1,950 rpm the average Maggie (including P6382) settles at a comfortable 110 mph and uses only about 6½ gal/hr to achieve it, but when fuel consumption is not critical the Gipsy Major will purr happily to give an IAS of 120 mph or more. Full throttle on the level produces a creditable 135 mph and in this condition the ailerons are satisfyingly responsive and sufficiently stiff to provide a pleasant feel of bite. In the type's later active days, in the early fifties, many a Maggie operated by Air Schools at Derby, Wolverhampton and Elstree used a Major 1c with aluminium-alloy cylinder heads, and this smartened the performance even more.

At the stall the Magister shows its colours. Clean, this occurs at about 52 mph IAS and a wing, nearly always the right, drops quite energetically; rapid response produces the desired answer immediately, but either a delay or the erroneous use of aileron sets up an incipient spin. With full flap, things are delayed to about 45 mph IAS and in this condition the stall tends to be a more level-winged affair.

Spinning is not performed today on Shuttleworth's preserved machine, but in training days the Maggie wound quickly and decisively into a steepish spin with a rapid rotation rate. As with nearly every military trainer, the type suffered in its early career and the inevitable fuselage strakes appeared, but with these fitted the machine recovered fairly rapidly if the rudder-pause-stick sequence was applied uncompromisingly. It would not tolerate half measures; it just went on spinning, with no marked change in attitude or rate, until someone did something about it.

Aerobatics are off the menu today, but in its time it went round a loop happily from 130-135 mph IAS, although if pulled too tightly or flown too slowly at the top it could behave like a junior Harvard and roll out without help from within. Slow rolls, however, were very hard work and called for a hand-foot co-ordination that I neither mustered nor mastered. A few specialists, such as the late C. A. Nepean Bishop, managed to perform elegant rolls in public but I never knew how. The particular problem was unique to the Magister, for through a strange design fault the elevators became decreasingly effective as rudder was applied, yet in the roll a fair ration of rudder was needed at a time when elevator response was essential. In milder, but equally convincing, form the condition can be demonstrated today from erect level flight; apply rudder, hold off bank with aileron and the nose will go down. Ease back to rectify. More rudder, more nose down and more backward stick pressure. The nose still goes down, but if the pedals are centralised the elevators immediately bite and the nose rushes upwards. Today, in view of 6382's increasing age, we do this very gingerly.

The clean glide at 70 mph is relatively flat, but the maximum take-off weight of 2,000 lbs. offers some momentum and a positive and steady descent can be set up with relatively little disturbance from gusts when compared with many light aircraft. Flaps, which may be lowered at 75 mph, originally stretched from immediately inboard of each aileron right across the underside of the fuselage, and the resulting barn door effect made it almost impossible to misjudge an approach on the high side; but with a low wing set so close to the ground at the trailing edge the cushion effect near the ground could be quite dramatic. In a crosswind landing on a hard runway, with no natural grass-type braking, the air would build up from one side and could find no escape, resulting in the inevitable wing lifting and consequent swing, followed by a ground loop. The undercarriage tubes were intentionally weak links to save trouble at the legs' roots in the spar, so frequently a Maggie would shed a leg or two and sit sadly in the middle of the aerodrome, but serious damage was rare and often a machine was jacked up, new legs were fitted and away it went.

To reduce the trouble some machines had their centre-section flaps fixed in the up position and P6382 has this pilot's bonus incorporated. This has helped also to reduce drag on an overshoot which, from ground level and in conditions of no wind, could use a fair distance before attaining a safe height for raising flaps.

The tail-down attitude is shallow, so the late stage of the round-out is through a relatively small angle. A misjudged hold-off and premature touchdown do not create a major bounce as a reaction generated by the undercarriage, which rides hard, but it can produce a comparable visual effect through ballooning. A flapless landing produces a pleasantly positive 'clunk' on contact with the ground, compared with the slight woolliness caused by the cushion of lowered flaps, but it tends to need a lot of aerodrome, as the clean design of an aerodynamically smooth cantilever monoplane causes a marked runway-consuming float. It is a safe bet to land in this manner, however, if doing so in a crosswind on a hard surface.

This report is based on a number of flights in the Collection's Magister P6382, which has refreshed some earlier memories of the type. Despite its relative youth as an active World War II trainer, used in the civil field for a few years after the war, the Maggie is a much rarer bird than is many an older type. One example is flying with the Strathallan Collection in Scotland and another is being restored to fly in due course in East Anglia, but a flight of three (in the air together one day?) is the most that the world can hope to muster in the years to come. By virtue of its claim as the founder of the era of monoplane trainers, it has a justified place in the records of aviation history; but it is enjoyable to fly, too, and for some that is almost equally important!

21 *The Gloster Gladiator*
Wing Commander R. F. Martin

In 1954 a generous and public spirited offer was made to the Gloster Aircraft Company by Mr. Vivian L. Bellamy, an ex Fleet Air Arm pilot who at that time was running an aircraft business at Southampton.

After the war, Mr. Bellamy had acquired from the Disposal Board a Gloster Gladiator, which he restored to flying condition and registered as G-AMRK. Foreseeing the long-term problems of ensuring the survival of this historic aeroplane, he was prepared to offer it to Glosters (plus another almost complete airframe and engine) for the token sum of £50, on the understanding that the company would continue to maintain it in flying condition.

In the event, this proposition required quite a bit of selling to the management, who were up to their ears in Javelin production. Eventually, however, the cheque was signed and the Gladiator squeezed into a corner of the production hangar at Brockworth.

Enthusiasm in the works knew no bounds and by the end of 1955 it had been agreed that the apprentice school could undertake a complete rebuild. Permission was obtained from the Air Ministry and Ministry of Civil Aviation to fly with pre-war R.A.F. and squadron markings and the Gladiator next flew in 1958 as K 8032.*

In 1960 came the sad news that Glosters would be closing down. Pride and interest in the Gladiator had by this time spread to the top echelons of Hawker Siddeley Aviation (the parent group) who not only agreed to present the aircraft to the Shuttleworth Collection, but also donated a sum of money at the same time to ensure its preservation in flying condition. It was handed over to Shuttleworth at R.A.E. Bedford on 25th November, 1960, but was not based at Old Warden until seven years later. (The other Gladiator, mentioned in the second paragraph, belongs to the Shuttleworth Collection and is on long loan to the Royal Naval Air Station at Yeovilton, where it is being restored, hopefully to fly again).

During the course of the last twenty years, a considerable number of pilots have had the opportunity of flying the 'Glad'. Circumstantially, most of them have been test pilots with experience of quite a number of different aircraft types. The standard comment after a first flight has almost always been .... 'the nicest aeroplane I've ever flown'. It is only fair to add that the majority had not flown the bi-plane Fury.

The Gladiator cockpit is very typical of the era. The pilot's seat is embedded amongst the exposed tubes of the fuselage structure, to which are bracketed the various controls and levers. His feet are supported on the rudder pedals by two aluminium trays as there is no cockpit floor. Anything dropped inadvertently disappears irretrievably into the tubes and control runs below. Unusually, both sides of the cockpit hinge down, giving good forward view while taxying, although of course the aircraft has still to be swung from side to side a bit. This was the first British single-seat fighter to have a sliding canopy. The hood is operated by a wheel sliding in a grooved track on the port side. Pushing the wheel down the track closes the hood, which must then be locked by tightening the wheel. The trick here is to set off with the wheel slackened back only half a turn, as the hood runs back if the push force is not maintained.

Level with the pilot's left knee are the flap controls, consisting of an UP/DOWN selector lever and a hand operated hydraulic pump. Also on the left is the elevator trim wheel with a curious rotating scale which revolves in the opposite direction to the hand wheel.

In the centre of the instrument panel is the old standard R.A.F. blind flying panel with its artificial horizon and directional gyro, A.S.I., altimeter, V.S.I. and turn and slip; below it are the compass and pneumatic brake pressure gauge. On the left side are the fuel cock, main tank fuel gauge, mag switches and oxygen regulator.

The brakes are pneumatic, using air from a bottle charged by

an engine-driven compressor; they are controlled by differential movement of the rudder bar in conjunction with a hand lever on the spade grip.

The engine is primed for starting by turning on the priming cock and pumping the Kigass, but care is needed not to overprime which can result in a fire in the intake. After priming, the starter mag and both main mags are switched on and the starter button pressed. The starter motor operates through a slipping clutch, which usually does just that as the engine comes on compression, so the drill is to kick the engine over compression by short jabs on the button. If priming has been correct, the engine usually fires up at the second or third compression. (The engine can be hand-cranked if need be.) For run-up a man on the tail is essential.

The automatic boost control fitted to the engine limits the maximum boost obtainable at full throttle to $+3\frac{1}{2}$lb. A device is incorporated, however, which permits the override of the boost control and allows an increase in the maximum boost obtainable to $+5$lb. This boost override is operated by the mixture control lever, the travel of the cockpit control being extended rearwards from the normal to a rich position. When the lever is moved fully back to this position, not only is the automatic boost control cut out, but the mixture is automatically enriched. A stop is incorporated in the automatic boost control system so that if it or its connections fail, there is always a minimum of engine power available. Obviously $+5$lb. boost is never used in our Shuttleworth flying and to conserve engine life even $+3\frac{1}{2}$lb. is used as little as possible.

Just below the throttle and mixture lever is a push-pull control for carburettor heat. The Mercury is extremely prone to carburettor icing and even on the most auspicious day this can occur. I hang my head in shame at forgetting this while ferrying the Gladiator from Staverton to Old Warden in 1975 after overhaul. Cruising at 3,000ft. below cumulus on a lovely summer's day, the engine died twenty minutes out. Only after unsuccessfully changing tanks and setting-up a forced landing did the proverbial penny drop.

The aeroplane is very easy to taxy, as it runs straight and can be steered mainly with the rudder and only an occasional touch of the brakes to assist. Whereas many earlier Shuttleworth aeroplanes have little more than trim (in some, not even that) and fuel to check, the Gladiator requires a more thorough set of 'vital actions' prior to take-off. The hood, side panels and harness must be locked, the elevator trim placed at zero and the flaps up. On the engine side the mixture control should be normal, the carburettor heat cold and the oil cooler normal, with the fuel selected to the gravity tank. After setting the gyros, compass and altimeter and checking the flying controls for full and free movement, the machine is ready to go.

There is no difficulty in keeping straight during take-off if the throttle is opened gently, but quite a large amount of rudder is necessary. The elevator control is powerful and care must be taken not to get the tail too high. The aircraft will fly off at 55-60 knots; climbing speed is 95 knots. As soon as the Gladiator is airborne the pilot starts to appreciate the good handling qualities. The three controls are beautifully harmonised, light and effective without being touchy. The aeroplane is statically stable, stick free, throughout the speed range, but stick forces to change speed are low, so one is not continually trimming during manoeuvres and its aerobatic qualities are delightful. In aerobatics we spare the 'G' as much as possible and flick manoeuvres and spins are forbidden.

With flaps up and half fuel the straight stall occurs 'off the clock' at around 45 knots and with the flaps down at a couple of knots less. There is no pre-stall buffet, but the aircraft stalls straight with a gentle nose drop and no tendency to drop a wing or spin.

The approach and landing present no problems. Speed is reduced in the circuit to below 78 knots which is the flap limiting speed. Flaps are selected and then pumped down by the hand pump, an operation taking less than ten seconds and producing a small nosedown change in trim. Pre-landing checks are fuel, brake pressure, mixture and carburettor heat, the only other consideration being to keep the engine reasonably warm on the descent. Final approach speed is 65 knots to cross the hedge at 55 for a three-point landing. Should one bounce, there is no tendency to drop a wing, but in cross-winds of more than 10 knots it is best to do a wheeler. There is only one thing I dislike when flying the Gladiator – getting out!

*(K was known not to be the authentic prefix, but as this aircraft was painted in the markings of No. 72 Squadron and an L serial would have been too late an issue, K was used. After its major overhaul in 1975 the Gladiator was repainted with its correct serial, which is L 8032.)

22 The Supermarine Spitfire Vc
Neil Williams

Of all the machines seen at air displays these days, perhaps the one that most captures the imagination is the Spitfire. It saw service throughout the Second Wolrd War in many theatres and was modified again and again for a particular role. Yet the hard facts of its career are only part of the story: it was symbolic of the victory over the Luftwaffe in 1940 which gave us the breathing space we needed to turn the tide of the war; and it was perhaps the most beautiful fighting aeroplane ever created.

AR 501 is a Spitfire Mk Vc, with clipped wings. It was brought back to flying condition for the film 'The Battle of Britain', a giant screen epic whose main claim to fame in the future will surely be that it called for several Spitfires to be restored to fly again; otherwise many would have rotted away. After the film was over, AR 501 was stored for three years and then was accepted at Duxford for restoration, and the result of years of painstaking work came to fruition on the day she was rolled out, authentically finished in the markings of No. 310 (Czech) squadron, with which she had served. Now she was to embark on the last stage of her career, as a flying historic aeroplane on the strength of the Shuttleworth Collection. But first she had, for the last time, to prove herself.

With trolley-acc in position, I climbed carefully onto the wing, trying not to scratch the paintwork, and eased myself into the cockpit, as clean and neat as was the rest of the machine. Electric power was available through a small switch on the throttle quadrant; this was automatically selected on when the throttle was opened. By late Spitfire standards, this was a simple cockpit: there was no idle-cut-off lever, no booster pump, not even a wobble pump; in effect, the cockpit was the same as a Spitfire I. I turned on the fuel, unscrewed the Ki-Gass pump and gave a few good shots. Throttle set, brakes locked on, stick back, mags on, and I pressed booster and starter buttons. The Merlin started easily, and settled into a smooth growl as I checked temperatures and pressures. The three-bladed metal propeller seemed to damp out some of the usual vibration, and this made the whole machine feel tight and smooth. With only one radiator, the coolant temperature rose rapidly, so that one had to be quick with the checks. I closed the hood and waved four mechanics onto the tail, to keep it from lifting. I opened up to full power, the slipstream hammering unmercifully at the ground crew, almost suffocating them in its ferocity. With the stick kicking and snatching in my hand I quickly scribbled down the engine figures, boost +9 lbs., rpm 2,700, and then, as the radiator temperature rose to 100°C I throttled back to let her cool. She was a little down on power but there was quite enough to do the test flight. I shut down while the mechanics inspected the engine for coolant or oil leaks, and then prepared to fly her.

Again the Merlin started easily, and already warm, was ready to go. I waved the chocks away, and with the seat raised high so that I could see past the cowling, I released the brakes and she moved under her own power. I taxyed slowly, but aware all the time of the mounting radiator temperature, in spite of the radiator shutter being wide open, the position of the shutter being shown by the control lever on the left of the cockpit. I completed the checks as I taxyed, making sure to tighten the throttle friction unit and remembering to wind on full right rudder trim to help compensate for the swing to the left on take-off. The temperature was rising as I turned onto the runway, and I lowered the seat and closed the hood. Now the growl of the Merlin was muted, and the acrid exhaust fumes no longer stung the eyes. I checked the brake pressure – still well up, because this Spitfire seemed to be able to taxy on rudder alone without needing the brakes – an unusual, but welcome, feature. With the tailwheel straight, I could no longer see ahead.

I increased power to 1,200 rpm and with the stick hard back, released the brakes. As she started to roll, I steadily applied power and eased the stick towards neutral, all the time alert for a sudden swing. As I reached full power, the tail came up quite quickly, unlike other Spitfires, and she accelerated rapidly with hardly any tendency to swing. She was still firmly on the ground, accelerating hard, at 90 mph, so I pulled steadily back on the stick until she unstuck. Quickly changing hands I moved the undercarriage lever inwards, upwards and forwards and finally outwards, whilst flying the aeroplane left handed. One used to be able to tell the novice Spitfire pilots because the aircraft used to pitch about when they changed hands, but perhaps even a novice could have flown AR 501 steadily: she was much more stable than usual. It is most important to check that the wheels are fully retracted; otherwise the right leg may hang down in front of the radiator and cause an overheating problem. Also, unlike modern aircraft, there is a window, coloured red, which is inscribed 'UP', but very often, due to micro-switch maladjustment, even when the gear is up the light can be out, so one then has to push the undercarriage lever fully forward for a couple of seconds to illuminate the red light and confirm gear up. When retraction is complete, a hydraulic circuit 'idle' flag appears in a window on the selector box.

While the undercarriage was retracting I throttled back to +6 lbs. boost, 2,650 rpm. I always use a back-handed grip on the pitch lever after the day, many years ago, when I nearly pulled back the idle-cut-off lever instead of the pitch lever! Although not all Spitfires have ICO levers, nowadays I make it a habit to hold the pitch lever back-handed. Meanwhile AR 501 was flying very steadily, and not trying to diverge in pitch as do most of her kind. As speed increased I was now holding left rudder pressure, so I had to back off quickly on the rudder trim. In common with all Spitfires, she would not tolerate the slightest hint of slipshod flying.

Now was also the time to ease off the throttle friction nut slightly: if it is not fully tight on take-off the throttle closes when one changes hands to retract the undercarriage – it only has to happen once – one never forgets the experience! As I reduced to cruising power of +4 lbs. boost/2,000 rpm and trimmed the aircraft, I noted the superb harmonisation; so much better with the clipped wings. In this machine one does not turn mechanically, one merely thinks of turning and it is done! She is instantly responsive, but touchy as a thorough-bred; even a slightly out-of-balance turn causes the pilot

to be ashamed of mishandling such a sensitive machine. The elevator trimmer is powerful, but the trim curve is fairly flat, so it is not necessary to make many adjustments. For every change of power and speed, however, the directional trim change is considerable. The view over the nose is much improved in flight, now that one at last has time to look around. As the radiator temperature falls, one can close off the radiator shutter: there is an optimum position, not quite fully closed, where the drag is lowest; this position is clearly marked alongside the control lever.

I was enthralled by the effect of the clipped wings; the aileron response was immediate and powerful, and they were much lighter than usual. Together with the reduced damping in roll, one could hardly resist the temptation to rock the aircraft gently from side to side merely to feel the instant control power. One could appreciate it all the more because of the excellent longitudinal stability: this Spitfire flew beautifully hands off for quite long periods. But there was work to be done: some performance figures had to be found. With the radiator shutter wide open and +6 lbs. 2,650 rpm set she arrowed upwards at a steady 3,000 feet per minute! With undercarriage and flaps down and the Merlin idling, I carried out a slow approach to the stall. As the speed dropped through 75 mph, I could quite clearly hear the airflow separating around the canopy, until, without further warning, she dropped her nose and left wing at 59 mph – slower than many modern light aeroplanes! She was fully controllable right into the stall, and there was plenty of elevator left even when she stalled – I would have no trouble rounding out on landing.

Now it was time to explore the high speed range. With the nose down she accelerated rapidly, the needle of the ASI soon showing 350 mph, which was quite fast enough with an old aeroplane. The controls were tight and hard, but the ailerons did not become really heavy as they do on round-winged Spitfires; she still retained her stability and harmonization. With no radio to intrude I could listen to the roar of the slipstream blending with the incomparable note of the Merlin. I eased out of the dive, and as the nose came up, the temptation was too much, and with the slightest pressure on the stick, she rolled effortlessly in the climb.

On such a powerful machine, one always has to be attentive

to two things; fuel consumption and navigation. At full power a Merlin can burn 130 gallons of fuel per hour, and one has only 85 gallons to start with! On the other hand, when flying for economy at −4 lbs. boost and 1,800 rpm, the consumption is reduced to 30 gallons per hour. At a cruising speed of 240 mph, the Spitfire covers the ground quickly, and with the network of controlled airspace which covers the country, one has to keep up with one's navigation. But with such an aeroplane one is reluctant to fly straight and level for long. Looping is easy, but requires a light touch on the stick – too much back pressure and she shudders on the edge of a stall. Over the top one needed accurate footwork to keep straight. It was hot, too, in this tiny cockpit, heavy with the smell of petrol and glycol. But all too soon, it was time to think of landing, so, reluctantly, I took her home. We levelled low over the runway, arcing up and around in a fighter break with the Merlin cracking its approval.

A curving approach, speed 100 mph, radiator flap open wide to cool that great engine, undercarriage light green, a hiss of air and a sudden trim shift as the flaps came down, and as the broad expanse of asphalt disappeared under the nose I throttled back fully and eased the stick back, flying now with finger tips. Over the hedge at 80 mph, she touched, gentle as a thistledown, running straight and true, the wheels taking the weight as she slowed. I braked carefully, for the brake power varies considerably from Spitfire to Spitfire. AR 501 has excellent brakes but in spite of this, her tail remained firmly on the ground. On later Spitfires with heavier engines one has to use the brakes with care, as it is only too easy to lift the tail, and the propeller clearance is minimal. As I taxyed back to dispersal I again found that I could taxy on rudder alone, even downwind, so that I needed brakes only to turn right corners. She had all the good qualities of the average Spitfire, and, it seemed, none of the less desirable ones. She handled so well on the approach, with a constant pull force on the stick as speed decreased, that one had the confidence to bring her in very slowly, which is necessary when landing at Old Warden.

In spite of the slightly forward centre of gravity and good brakes, she stops quickly without lifting the tail. Her excellent handling, both on the ground and in the air, are due to this forward C.G., which, together with her clipped wings and powerful ailerons, make her by far the most rewarding Spitfire

I have flown. Her appearance and behaviour are a tribute to the enthusiasts who worked on her so long and so hard. They may well be proud of her.

Aircraft operation – 1914/18
Wing Commander T. E. Guttery

Wing Commander T. E. Guttery was in the Royal Flying Corps before the start of World War I. Because of his experience on the technical side from the very earliest days of Service aviation, we have asked him to write this special report.

The aeroplane as an instrument of mechanical flight had no more than demonstrated its potentiality than its adaptation as a war weapon brought into being naval and military air services. That of Great Britain in 1912 became the Royal Flying Corps comprising Naval and Military Wings; the naval arm in early 1914 becoming the Royal Naval Air Service. Some of the oldest of the Collection's aeroplanes are of the era that ended with these Services reverting to a unity that became the Royal Air Force; it is to this period that the following applies.

The aeroplanes of this period were essentially light structures depending for flight on engines of limited power and reliability, their vulnerability to damage and derangement being such as to require painstaking attention to the handling, inspection and scrutiny of detail. They were uncomplicated structures; details of their construction, operation of their controls, care and treatment of the materials employed being such that a craftsman of reasonable intelligence and skill needed little tuition to become competent in the effective maintenance and handling of the aeroplane proper, or what later became known as the airframe. A qualified motor mechanic was equally capable of acquiring the knowledge essential for the care and handling of the engine. The instruments then used were based on types in universal use and unlikely to give false readings or to need specialized knowledge: revolution counter, bourdon tube operated pressure gauges, baragraph of the altimeter and spirit level of the inclinometer.

In these circumstances a maintenance crew consisted only of these two individuals who were known respectively as Rigger and Fitter. Normally a crew of this composition was allocated to each aeroplane. In a flying unit or squadron, as distinct from a training establishment, each aeroplane had its own pilot, he and his crew forming an interdependant entity or team. Squadrons normally were of twelve aeroplanes which were subdivided into alphabetically designated sections called flights, each being of four aeroplanes and commanded by a Flight Commander. Supervision of aeroplane care and maintenance was the responsibility of non-commissioned officers, the whole technical control being overseen by a technical warrant officer.

Before proceeding further it should be stated that hand-books descriptive of aeroplanes which later became customary were non-existent, such information as was available being limited to specifications with drawings giving dimensional and rigging details. Technical notes for the various types were later produced by Service sources. Descriptive handbooks for engines were usually supplied, but some of these were produced by Service personnel after attending instructional courses at manufacturers' works.

The essential service of inspection was at that time without the guidance of the latter-day inspection schedules, the needs of this exercise being plainly apparent to the crew which, with the advice of the supervisory staff, was fully competent. The average undisrupted life of the early aeroplanes was so short and the kind of repairs entailed by unserviceability arising such that periodical inspection of the major and minor variety that later became regularized had never become a need, the aeroplane's subsequent serviceability having been achieved thereby.

With regard to the inspections referred to, the stresses imposed by taxying, flight operation and landing with structures of this nature and engine wear and tear, service-ability could only be assured by a rigidly applied system of pre, inter and after flight inspection. Broadly these entailed examination of control and other surfaces for distortion, wires for tension and maladjustment, locking of twinbuckles, control wires for tension, wear and lubrication, at pulley locations in particular, undercarriage and tail skid for alignment, condition of tyres and shock absorber elastics. Cleanliness, treatment against corrosion and so on were, of course, essentials. Pilots would report any occasion needing special 'after flight' inspection.

Responsibility for the satisfactory operation of aeroplanes rested solely on the Commanding Officer of the squadron. Any action in this connection that was not already apparent and where safety was involved (and mostly such actions were arrived at empirically) was made the subject of orders which were communicated to all concerned, rigidly enforced and given a regular place at what was later to become the 'Flight Desk'. Documents needed for this purpose were locally improvised and their purport acknowledged by the signatures of all concerned. This system applied to the serviceability of aeroplanes, authorisation of flights and similar authorisations and certifications. It was by these means rather than by the standardized and universally applied systems currently in use that responsibility was apportioned and compliance certified. Information from this source essential to the historical record of the aeroplane or its engine, together with any necessary certification, was recorded in their respective log books. These details supplemented those of times and duration of flights and those of quantities of fuel and oil replenishments.

Aerodromes, or airfields as they later became known, were of grass carefully selected having regard to surface, freedom from external features likely to cause air currents or obstruction, freedom to land in any direction, unavoidable obstructions, with hangars, for instance, so orientated as to allow the longest run in the direction of the prevailing wind.

The general well-being and safety of the aeroplane owed much to the care and treatment given to its handling on the ground. Its housing normally ensured its protection against moisture and dampness. When not in use it was supported by trestles or other means so as to relieve its tyres and shock absorbers from supporting its weight. Supports of this kind were arranged only at such points as would not subject members to any bending or distortion. Movement of the aeroplane normally was facilitated by the employment of a tail trolley which gave support by engaging the tail skid, thereby not only taking the weight but, in movement, controlling its direction. Movement was also further assisted either by pulling or pushing from the undercarriage or from the base of interplane struts. Care was taken to ensure that inexperienced helpers only applied pressure at these points. Fire precautions were a normal provision. In the event of an aeroplane having to be left out in the open it was always placed to face the wind; when the weather was windy controls were well secured against movement. In all cases it was customary to use engine and cockpit covers.

In moving aeroplanes in and out of hangars, care was needed to avoid obstructions of any kind and in all cases involving movement this was supervised either by an officer or non-commissioned officer so placed as to be able to view the action as a whole. In movements over the airfield, obstacles and holes had to be avoided; where effort was needed to relieve weight or resistance to movement, care had to be taken to apply pressure only at points capable of sustaining it. Directional control of aircraft when taxying was impossible of achievement by rudder, but needed the assistance of mechanics at wing tips to effect turning movement. This sort of assistance was also necessary when taxying in a strong wind.

Aeroplanes were normally certified as serviceable before leaving the hangar, fully replenished with fuel and oil, with subsequent preparation for flight usually undertaken adjacent to the hangar provided the running up of the engine would create no disturbance through blast from the propeller. At this point the aeroplane was inspected by the pilot who satisfied himself that all was in order. Runways were not of the period, so direction of flight or the position at which preparation was made was so selected as would be most advantageous from the take-off point of view; movement to effect this was by means already mentioned. The procedure for starting the engine was based on a standard and clear intercommunication code by which starting has been conducted with safety and effectiveness and this procedure has remained current.

The stationary engines of the Collection's aeroplanes are based on the same principles and run in exactly the same way as the ordinary motor car engine; since, however, the rotary engines are intrinsically different in this respect a brief explanatory note may enlighten the uninformed reader. Of the engines powering the Collection's aeroplanes, control of the rotary types is the most onerous: they have no carburettor in the ordinary sense, the combustible mixture being provided by a device getting its air and fuel from independent sources, with the proportion of the mixture being under the control of the pilot rather than being adjusted by the float chamber jet combination of the conventional carburettor. Fuel and air are governed by fluid and gas laws, this difference resulting in the supply of more fuel than air as engine speed increases, so correct proportioning of the mixture is made by a pilot-operated mixture control which needs expert adjustment. Having made adjustment for normal flying, substantial reduction of power (as needed when landing or taxying) is best achieved by switching the engine on and off, for which a thumb operated push-button switch on the control column is normally provided.

As a matter of interest the advent of the rotary engine resulted from the inability to achieve much progress in mechanical flight due to the weight penalty imposed by such conventional type engines as were then available or undergoing development. By holding the crankshaft stationary, thereby allowing the remainder of the engine to rotate about it, not only eliminated the need for a flywheel but overcame cooling problems: by this means the weight/power ratio was reduced by at least a half. Although extravagant in fuel and oil consumption it contributed more to the progress of aviation of its period than any other type of engine. 70% of the aircraft exhibited at the 1913 Paris Aero Salon and 80% of those competing in the British Aerial Derby of that year were powered by rotary engines.

The aircraft is first positioned with its head to the wind; checks against forward movement of the aeroplane are provided in most cases by devices called wheel chocks, one being placed in front of each wheel. Attached to one side of each is a rope, these being so arranged that their attachments face inwards to each other; then the ropes are carried to the wing tips of their sides, thereby facilitating their easy removal from the wheels by a tug on the ropes.

Procedure to be followed in starting the various types of engine, though different, have many points in common: in the interests of brevity they will be generalized where possible. The methods of starting can first be described as follows: (1) Swinging of the propeller by hand, which can be either a swing by one person or by two or more by joining hands. (2) By starting magneto. (3) By swinging with use of starting magneto. (4) By independent mechanical starter, e.g. Hucks. (5) By self-starter.

The number of mechanics normally engaged in the process take up positions one at each wing tip, one at the tail and the number needed for the swinging or otherwise to rotate the propeller. Those at the wing tips take up the chock ropes and keep their eyes on the pilot; where swinging is employed those concerned should make sure that their foothold is sound, and that they are not wearing any loose articles of clothing. Before touching the propeller at all they must be sure that the engine switches are off.

Having taken his seat and being in communication with his mechanics the pilot exchanges coded terms as follows. In the case of the rotary engine, the pilot when ready to start calls 'Switches off, petrol on', the starting mechanic replies 'Switches off, petrol on'; turning the engine until one cylinder is at the bottom with its exhaust valve open, he then calls 'petrol off' as soon as he sees petrol issuing from the cylinder. Pilot replies 'petrol off', mechanic turns propeller for a few revolutions and leaves in swinging position: he then stands clear and calls 'contact', pilot replies 'contact' and switches on, mechanic swings and pilot turns on petrol when engine starts.

In the case of other engines with no other starting mechanism the pilot first calls 'switch off, petrol on, suck in'; the mechanic replies in similar terms and then rotates the propeller sufficiently to induce a charge, then, standing clear, he calls 'contact'. The pilot replies 'contact' and mechanic swings propeller.

Where a Hucks starter is used, precisely the same terms are used except that after connecting up the starter shaft to the propeller, stands clear and calls 'all clear', thereby allowing the starter operator to act as the swinger. Where a hand starting magneto is used in conjunction with swinging, the pilot calls 'swinging contact' and the mechanic ready to swing calls 'one, two, three go' and swings, whereupon the starter is manipulated.

Failure to start in either of these cases usually calls for a repetition of these actions; failing this it may be necessary to inject fuel, or colloquially to 'dope', into the cylinder or induction system; if on the other hand the mixture is too rich the propeller is turned backwards two or three revolutions partially to clear the cylinders before repeating the starting action. In these cases the code word exchanged is 'reverse' or sometimes 'blow out'.

After starting, the engine can now be run at suitable revolutions to warm up, during which time the appropriate engine instruments are checked for normal readings; after this the pilot signals his readiness to move, when the chocks are pulled away by the wing tip mechanic and, after what guidance is needed from the ground staff, the pilot is free to take the air. That all is clear is jointly acknowledged by the exchange of salutes between pilot and senior member of staff.

On completion of the flight the aeroplane is handled by the crew following the principles already defined. This is followed by after flight inspection and refuelling as necessary.

The rapid development of the aeroplane and the evolutionary advancement of servicing procedures demanded thereby progressively brought into being a high degree of standardisation. Regulations for the newly instituted Royal Air Force and Air Council Instructions made unit commanders responsible for promulgating Unit Maintenance (later servicing) Orders in which Part I described the responsibilities of individuals, servicing and organization procedures and Part II Inspection Schedules. The Air Ministry also introduced standard documents called Weekly Aircraft Maintenance Form 535 and, in 1936, finalized these arrangements by issuing Air Publication 1574 (Aeroplane Maintenance Regulations) which brought into use an elaborately conceived Form 700. These and the variety of instructional manuals now available take into account all the contingencies dealt with in the foregoing.

About the Pilots

(To avoid the need for repetition, note that all learnt to fly while serving with the Royal Air Force.)

Wing Commander Roland Prosper Beamont, C.B.E.: Born 1920. Educated Eastbourne College. Joined Royal Air Force 1938. Shot down 10 enemy aircraft and 32 flying bombs. Awarded D.S.O. and bar; D.F.C. and bar. Attached as test pilot to Hawker Aircraft 1941; joined Gloster Aircraft 1945. Chief Test Pilot for English Electric 1947-61. Flew first British jet bomber (Canberra) 1949 and first British supersonic jet fighter (P.1 Lightning) 1954. Pilot of first British aircraft to exceed Mach 2 (Lightning) 1958. Pilot of Britain's first supersonic bomber (TSR 2) 1964. Now Director of Flight Operations, Military Aircraft Division of British Aircraft Corporation at Preston.

Wing Commander Thomas Ewart Guttery, M.B.E., C.Eng., M.R.Ae.S.: Born December 3rd 1894. Educated Brierley Hill. Royal Flying Corps No. 3 and 5 Squadrons. British Expeditionary Force 1912: 1914 World War I. Produced first Service built BE2c fitting with effective dual control, designed and incorporated dual control conversions Sopwith Camel and Dolphin, introduced production line system for aircraft repair inviting liaison Institute of Industrial Administration. Between Wars, Technical Training School, Repair Depots, Flying Station, Commanded Mechanical Transport and marine craft squadron, Central Trade Test Board, World War II. Introduced training in Instrument repairs for W.R.A.F., senior staff appointment Training Command, loaned to Air Ministry for investigation maintenance R.C.A.F. Directorate of Repair and Maintenance, Engines, Ministry of Aviation Production

Post War. Senior Technical Staff Officer No. 46 and No. 38 (Airborne Forces) Groups Transport Command. Directorate of Technical Training Air Ministry. After retirement 1950 special appointment R.A.F. Technical College; staff appointment Bomber Command 1961. Honorary post Shuttleworth Collection. Writer of publications, research, etc.

John Telford Scott Lewis: Born in London, 1937, but raised in Scotland. Graduated from Royal Air Force College, Cranwell, 1958, and flew Canberras in Middle East. Won three of four course trophies at Central Flying School 1962. Chief Flying Instructor, Oxford University Air Squadron 1963. Won Patuxent shield on Empire Test Pilots' School Course 1966. O.C. Aerodynamics Research Flight at R.A.E. Bedford, and awarded A.F.C. in 1972. Resigned as Squadron Leader to join Rolls-Royce (1971) Ltd. Now Deputy Chief Test Pilot, involved with development of power-plant installations in fixed and rotary-winged types. Lives near Bristol. Interests include railways, music, motor-cycles and cats.

Wing Commander Richard Frewen Martin: Born 1918, educated Cheltenham. Graduated from Royal Air Force College, Cranwell, 1939, where he won the Groves Memorial flying prize, then to 75 Squadron on Hurricanes at Digby. Wartime service in U.K., France, Middle East and India; awarded D.F.C. and Bar. Flew 'the Hump' in 1946, before posting to Empire Test Pilots' School; commanded Aero Flight at Farnborough, Tutor at E.T.P.S. and awarded A.F.C. Graduated from Royal Air Force Flying College, Manby, 1951. Staff Officer Air Ministry 1951-52, retiring at own request to join Gloster Aircraft Co. as Chief Test Pilot in 1953. After G.A.C. closure in 1960, with Armstrong Whitworth at Bitteswell on Argosy development and then with Avro at Manchester on Vulcan, Shackleton, and 748 programmes. Awarded O.B.E. and Queen's Commendation. Joined Autair (later Courtline) in 1968 as Training Captain on 748, and B.A.C.1-11. Following Courtline collapse, training Advisor to Air Malawi 1974-75. Hobby: hot air ballooning.

David Frederick Ogilvy: Born 1929. Educated Aldenham. Flew Mosquitos on 58 Squadron. Chief Flying Instructor, Elstree, from 1952, becoming Director of London and Midland Schools of Flying and Chief Instructor, Air Schools, until 1966. Flew in most U.K. air races, 1950-56, mainly in

Avro Cadet and Comper Swift. Currently a Director of the Aircraft Owners' and Pilots' Association; member of Council, the Transport Trust; Vice Chairman, British Aircraft Preservation Council; member of U.K. General Aviation Safety Committee; Vice Chairman, Aerodrome Operators' Committee; editor of 'BLAC Manual of Flying and Ground Training'; author of 'Flying Facts', 'Flying Light Aircraft' and 'Discovering Old Aeroplanes'. General Manager of the Shuttleworth Collection since 1966. Interests include railways, wildfowl, choral singing and cycling.

John Desmond Penrose: Born 1930, educated Loughborough College. Member of Nottingham University Air Squadron. Served in Egypt 1952-55 with 208 Squadron. Winner Clarkson Aerobatic Trophy at Central Flying School 1955. Instructed at Cranwell before course at Empire Test Pilots' School 1958. Test Pilot at Royal Aircraft Establishment, Farnborough, before resigning to join de Havillands as development test pilot 1961, initially on HS 125 and later Trident. Pilot of first Trident delivered to People's Republic of China. Instrument rating examiner, type rating examiner on Trident HS 125 and Dove. Now flight operations manager with United Air Service of Lagos, Nigeria. As yet unfulfilled ambition: to fly a Spitfire.

Air Commodore Allen Henry Wheeler: Educated Eton and Cambridge, where he obtained an engineering degree. Learnt to fly in 1925 on Avro 504K's and then flew Bristol Fighters on army co-operation duties. Individual Aerobatic Display Pilot at R.A.F. Pageant 1927. Commanded experimental Flying Dept. at R.A.E. Farnborough, and the Airborne Forces Experimental Establishment at Beaulieu; took part in D-day invasion of Normandy, and operations over Arnhem, while commanding R.A.F. Fairford. Final posting, before retirement in 1955, was Head of Experimental Establishment at Boscombe Down. Has owned S.E.5A and two Spitfires. Aviation Technical Advisor for films 'Those Magnificent Men in their Flying Machines' and 'The Blue Max' and author of 'That Nothing Failed Them' (about experimental flying in 1939-45 war), 'Building Aeroplanes for those Magnificent Men' and 'Flying Between the Wars'. In 1975 celebrated 50 years of flying as a pilot. Aviation Trustee of the Richard Ormonde Shuttleworth Remembrance Trust.

Neil Williams: Born in Calgary, Canada, 1934, and educated in Wales. Joined Royal Air Force in 1955 and trained with Royal Canadian Air Force in Canada. Flew Canberras in Middle East before course at Empire Test Pilots' School 1962. Experimental test pilot at Farnborough before leaving Royal Air Force 1967 to join Handley Page on Jetstreams. Co-founder of Rothman's Aerobatic Team 1970. European Aerobatic Champion 1967-1969. Currently British Aerobatic Champion for 12th time. Captain of British Aerobatic Team since 1966. Awarded Queen's Commendation for landing aerobatic aircraft after mid-air structural failure. Author of 'Aerobatics' and regular contributor to aviation magazines. Now self-employed as freelance pilot for test and de-monstration flying, ferrying, film and charter work.